Genetic Engineering

Other Books of Related Interest:

At Issue Series

DNA Databases

Genetically Engineered Food

Should Parents Be Allowed to Choose the Sex
of Their Children?

Introducing Issues with Opposing
Viewpoints Series

Endangered Species

Opposing Viewpoints Series

Cloning

Stem Cells

GLOBALVIEWPOINTS

Genetic Engineering

Noah Berlatsky, Book Editor

GREENHAVEN PRESS
A part of Gale, Cengage Learning

GALE
CENGAGE Learning·

Detroit • New York • San Francisco • New Haven, Conn • Waterville, Maine • London

Elizabeth Des Chenes, *Director, Publishing Solutions*

© 2013 Greenhaven Press, a part of Gale, Cengage Learning

Gale and Greenhaven Press are registered trademarks used herein under license.

For more information, contact:
Greenhaven Press
27500 Drake Rd.
Farmington Hills, MI 48331-3535
Or you can visit our Internet site at gale.cengage.com

For product information and technology assistance, contact us at

Gale Customer Support, 1-800-877-4253
For permission to use material from this text or product, submit all requests online at www.cengage.com/permissions

Further permissions questions can be emailed to permissionrequest@cengage.com

Articles in Greenhaven Press anthologies are often edited for length to meet page requirements. In addition, original titles of these works are changed to clearly present the main thesis and to explicitly indicate the author's opinion. Every effort is made to ensure that Greenhaven Press accurately reflects the original intent of the authors. Every effort has been made to trace the owners of copyrighted material.

Cover image © Nigel Cattlin/Alamy.

LIBRARY OF CONGRESS CATALOGING-IN-PUBLICATION DATA

Genetic engineering / Noah Berlatsky, book editor.
    p. cm. -- (Global viewpoints)
    Summary: "Genetic Engineering: Global Viewpoints examines current, often controversial, topics of worldwide interest and importance from a variety of international perspectives"-- Provided by publisher.
    Includes bibliographical references and index.
    ISBN 978-0-7377-6265-5 (hardback) -- ISBN 978-0-7377-6441-3 (paperback)
    1. Genetic engineering--Juvenile literature. 2. Genetic engineering--Social aspects--Juvenile literature. 3. Genetic engineering--Environmental aspects--Juvenile literature. 4. Food--Biotechnology--Juvenile literature. I. Berlatsky, Noah.
    QH442.G4412 2012
    660.6'5--dc23

                                                              2012009956

Printed in Mexico
1 2 3 4 5 6 7 16 15 14 13 12

Contents

Chapter 1: Genetic Engineering and Crops

As the threat from climate change increases, China must develop new genetically modified (GM) crops to protect its food security and to reduce its reliance on foreign technology.

Chapter 2: Genetic Engineering and Disease

Chapter 3: Genetic Engineering and Animals

Scientists have had some success in cloning extinct animals. Cloning may be a valuable tool in conservation of extinct or endangered species, along with other measures.

Chapter 4: Genetic Engineering in Humans

Foreword

"The problems of all of humanity can only be solved by all of humanity."
—Swiss author Friedrich Dürrenmatt

Global interdependence has become an undeniable reality. Mass media and technology have increased worldwide access to information and created a society of global citizens. Understanding and navigating this global community is a challenge, requiring a high degree of information literacy and a new level of learning sophistication.

Building on the success of its flagship series, Opposing Viewpoints, Greenhaven Press has created the Global Viewpoints series to examine a broad range of current, often controversial topics of worldwide importance from a variety of international perspectives. Providing students and other readers with the information they need to explore global connections and think critically about worldwide implications, each Global Viewpoints volume offers a panoramic view of a topic of widespread significance.

Drugs, famine, immigration—a broad, international treatment is essential to do justice to social, environmental, health, and political issues such as these. Junior high, high school, and early college students, as well as general readers, can all use Global Viewpoints anthologies to discern the complexities relating to each issue. Readers will be able to examine unique national perspectives while, at the same time, appreciating the interconnectedness that global priorities bring to all nations and cultures.

Material in each volume is selected from a diverse range of sources, including journals, magazines, newspapers, nonfiction books, speeches, government documents, pamphlets, organization newsletters, and position papers. Global Viewpoints is truly global, with material drawn primarily from international sources available in English and secondarily from US sources with extensive international coverage.

Features of each volume in the Global Viewpoints series include:

- An **annotated table of contents** that provides a brief summary of each essay in the volume, including the name of the country or area covered in the essay.

- An **introduction** specific to the volume topic.

- A **world map** to help readers locate the countries or areas covered in the essays.

- For each viewpoint, an **introduction** that contains notes about the author and source of the viewpoint explains why material from the specific country is being presented, summarizes the main points of the viewpoint, and offers three **guided reading questions** to aid in understanding and comprehension.

- **For further discussion** questions that promote critical thinking by asking the reader to compare and contrast aspects of the viewpoints or draw conclusions about perspectives and arguments.

- A worldwide list of **organizations to contact** for readers seeking additional information.

- A **periodical bibliography** for each chapter and a **bibliography of books** on the volume topic to aid in further research.

- A comprehensive **subject index** to offer access to people, places, events, and subjects cited in the text, with the countries covered in the viewpoints highlighted.

Global Viewpoints is designed for a broad spectrum of readers who want to learn more about current events, history, political science, government, international relations, economics, environmental science, world cultures, and sociology—students doing research for class assignments or debates, teachers and faculty seeking to supplement course materials, and others wanting to understand current issues better. By presenting how people in various countries perceive the root causes, current consequences, and proposed solutions to worldwide challenges, Global Viewpoints volumes offer readers opportunities to enhance their global awareness and their knowledge of cultures worldwide.

Introduction

> *"With just one injection, an HIV/AIDS gene vaccine [may eventually be developed that] could replace the costly and often ineffective antiretroviral therapies now in use. Would anyone say, "We should not introduce this vaccine because it crosses the line between treatment and [genetic] enhancement . . . ?"*
>
> —*Ronald M. Green,*
> Babies by Design:
> The Ethics of Genetic Choice,
> *2007, p. 62*

Acquired immunodeficiency syndrome (AIDS), caused by the human immunodeficiency virus (HIV), is a disease that attacks the human immune system. It is transmitted from person to person through bodily fluids obtained from blood transfusion or through sexual contact. AIDS has had a major worldwide impact, especially in Africa. According to the international AIDS charity AVERT, as of the end of 2009, there were 33.3 million people worldwide living with AIDS or HIV. AVERT says there were 1.8 million AIDS deaths in 2009, and 2.6 million people newly infected with the disease.

Some discredited conspiracy theorists have argued that the AIDS epidemic was the result of deliberate genetic engineering. According to Juliet Lapidos in a March 19, 2008, article in *Slate*, one of the most popular genetic engineering AIDS conspiracy theories was suggested by Gary Glum. In his book *Full Disclosure*, Glum said that American scientists engineered AIDS, and that it was then spread by the World Health Organization through smallpox vaccines in order to wipe out the black population of the world. Another theory, according to

Lapidos, includes the claim that the AIDS virus was created by the United States with help from pharmaceutical company Merck and spread through a hepatitis B vaccine given primarily to gay men. A third theory suggests that AIDS was developed from a sheep virus and injected into prison inmates.

These theories are based on no evidence and have been thoroughly refuted by scientists and health workers. However, they have remained popular. James Hall, writing in the *Swazi Observer* on June 29, 2011, noted that fully 20 percent of South Africans between the ages of twenty and twenty-nine in Cape Town believed that scientists created the AIDS virus. Hall argues that this belief in conspiracy theories is dangerous because those who believe AIDS was genetically engineered often refuse to get tested for HIV. They may also refuse to wear condoms during sex, which is one of the best ways to prevent transmission of the disease. "The people who believe in the conspiracy are adopting a tone of apathy, and are acting like they are helpless to fight the conspiracy, when in fact all they would have to do is put on a condom," Hall wrote.

Though it cannot be proven that genetic engineering caused AIDS, some scientists hope that it might help to find a cure. Scientists have speculated for some time about possible ways of using genetic engineering to fight AIDS. In March 2003, for example, *Science in Africa* reported that Nobel Prize–winning scientist David Baltimore suggested that in fighting AIDS human beings' "natural immunity is too limited for our needs; we need to augment it with modern-day genetic engineering." Baltimore hoped to engineer a more effective antibody that could destroy the HIV virus.

Recently there have been some successful experiments in using genetic engineering to combat AIDS. According to Marilynn Marchione in a February 28, 2011, article on MSNBC, some researchers were inspired by the case of a person who had natural immunity to AIDS. The individual with immunity donated blood to a German AIDS patient, and the patient seemed to be cured of AIDS. Working from this example, scientists decided to use genetic engineering to develop blood cells resistant to HIV. The method was tried on six patients, and tests indicated that the procedure was safe, though its effectiveness has not yet been demonstrated. Carl Dieffenbach, the AIDS chief at the National Institute of Allergy and Infectious Diseases, was quoted as saying, "We're hopeful that this is sufficient to give the level of immune reconstitution similar to what was seen with the patient from Germany."

Scientists have also used genetic engineering in other ways to combat AIDS. According to Charles Q. Choi in a September 13, 2011, report on FOX News, researchers have genetically manipulated cats to carry a molecule that may help prevent AIDS. To make sure that the genetic information is transmitted correctly, the researchers also gave the cats a fluorescent jellyfish protein. Thus, the cats glow in the dark if the genetic material in question has been successfully passed to them.

Cats have been experiencing their own AIDS pandemic very similar to that of humans, making them good subjects for AIDS research. Eventually, researcher Eric Poeschla said, the research could prevent millions of cats from dying: "Supporting this research can help cats as much as people."

While some scientists have argued that genetic engineering can help advance the cause of AIDS research, others have worried that it may cause new perils. For example, in 1987, a team at the National Institutes of Health managed to place the AIDS virus genome in mice. Some scientists argued this would enable useful research. But, others disagreed, according to Linda Tagliaferro in her book *Genetic Engineering: Progress or Peril?* In particular, scientist Dr. Robert Gallo worried that the AIDS virus might combine with mouse viruses to create an even stronger and more dangerous kind of AIDS. Even if the AIDS virus did not mutate, Tagliaferro argued, the mice could be dangerous. If mice with AIDS genes escaped from the lab, and if they passed the AIDS virus in their genes on to their offspring, they might become a dangerous new means of spreading the AIDS virus among humans.

The remainder of this book looks at other issues and controversies surrounding genetic engineering in chapters titled Genetic Engineering and Crops, Genetic Engineering and Disease, Genetic Engineering and Animals, and Genetic Engineering in Humans. Different writers offer different viewpoints regarding the promises and perils of genetic engineering.

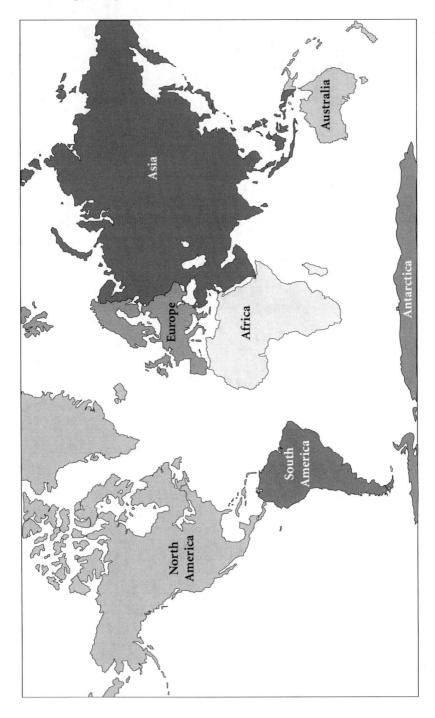

GLOBAL VIEWPOINTS

CHAPTER 1

Genetic Engineering and Crops

Genetically Modified Crops Can Prevent World Hunger

Henry Miller

Henry Miller is a physician, a molecular biologist, and a fellow in scientific philosophy and public policy at Stanford University's Hoover Institution. In the following viewpoint, he argues that unnecessary and unscientific regulations on genetically modified (GM) food drive up prices and discourage research and innovation. He argues that GM crops could help prevent world hunger and could provide new sources of biofuels that are not dependent on food crops. However, he says current public policy that places unnecessary regulations on GM crops stymies innovation. If public policy is not changed, he concludes, more people will go hungry.

As you read, consider the following questions:

1. What is one reason Miller gives for rising food prices in 2011?

2. According to Miller, how much of their food crops do the United States and Europe divert to the use of biofuels?

3. How many hungry people will there be worldwide by 2050 if food policy is not changed, according to the viewpoint?

Food prices worldwide were up by a whopping 25% in 2010, according to the UN's [United Nation's] Food and Agriculture Organization, and February [2011] marked the eighth consecutive month of rising global food prices. Within the past two months, food riots helped to trigger the ousting of ruling regimes in Tunisia and Egypt. (It is noteworthy that food prices increased 17% last year in Egypt, and the price of wheat, a critical staple there, soared by more than 50%.) For poor countries that are net importers of food, even small increases in food prices can be catastrophic, and recent bumps have been anything but small.

Causes of Rising Prices

There are several causes of rising prices. First, large-scale disasters have precipitated localised crop failures, some of which have had broad ripple effects—for example, Russia's ban on grain exports through at least the end of this calendar year resulted from fires and drought. Second, deadly strains of an evolving wheat pathogen (a rust) named Ug99 are increasingly threatening yields in the major wheat-growing areas of southern and eastern Africa, the central Asian republics, the Caucasus, the Indian subcontinent, South America, Australia and North America. Third, rising incomes in emerging markets like China and India have increased the ability of an expanding middle class to shift from a grain-based diet to one that contains more meat. [Editor's note: Cattle farming requires more grain than growing crops for human consumption. Therefore, more meat eaters means less grain overall.]

And fourth, against this backdrop of lessened supply and heightened demand, private investment in R&D [research and development] on innovative practices and technologies has been discouraged by arbitrary and unscientific national and international regulatory barriers—against, in particular, new varieties of plants produced with modern genetic engineering (aka recombinant DNA technology or genetic modification, or

GM). Genetic engineering offers plant breeders the tools to make crops do spectacular new things. In more than two dozen countries, farmers are using genetically engineered crop varieties to produce higher yields, with lower inputs and reduced impact on the environment.

Unscientific Barriers

But exploiting this advanced technology has been a tough row to hoe. Regulation commonly discriminates specifically against the use of the newest, most precise genetic engineering techniques, subjecting field trials to redundant case-by-case reviews and markedly inflating R&D costs. A veritable alphabet soup of United Nations' agencies and programmes are prime offenders, perpetuating a regulatory approach that is both unscientific and obstructionist. These public policy failures, in turn, inhibit the adoption and diffusion of new plants that boast a broad spectrum of new high value–added input and output traits.

Can the flawed public policy that prevails in most of the world be rationalised? Nina [V.] Fedoroff, professor of biology at Pennsylvania State University, former State Department senior adviser and currently visiting professor at King Abdullah University in Saudi Arabia, is not optimistic:

> The continuing distaste for [genetically engineered plants] and their consequent absurd over-regulation means that the most up-to-date, environmentally benign crop protection strategies are used almost exclusively for the mega-crops that are profitable for biotech companies. The public agricultural research sector remains largely excluded from using modern molecular technology. Will this change soon? I don't think so.

Fedoroff continues:

> The screams of pain will come first from the poorest countries that already import way beyond their ability to pay and

[are] too poor (or perhaps unwise) to make the requisite investments in developing new high-tech approaches to agriculture in hot places. And now we're pouring our ag [agriculture] bucks into biofuels [fuels made from biological materials], of all the imaginable absurdities.

In fact, the United States and Europe are diverting vast and increasing amounts of land and agricultural production into making ethanol [a fuel that can be made from common crops such as sugar cane and corn]. The United States is approaching the diversion of 40% of the corn harvest for fuel and the EU [European Union] has a goal of 10% biofuel use by 2020. The implications are worrisome. On 9 February, the US Department of Agriculture reported that the ethanol industry's projected orders for 2011 rose 8.4%, to 13.01bn bushels, leaving the United States with about 675m bushels of corn left at the end of the year. That is the lowest surplus level since 1996.

Discriminatory regulation has been complemented by outright antagonism to genetically engineered crops from antitechnology, antibusiness NGOs [nongovernmental organisations], and some governments.

If only the ingenuity of genetic engineers were unleashed, we would likely see innovative approaches to the production of energy from nonfood organisms, including switchgrass, trees and algae. But as Steven Strauss, professor at Oregon State University and an expert in genetic engineering of plants, has pointed out, regulators' approach to such sources of energy make field trials and commercialisation unfeasible.

Related to this issue is that discriminatory regulation has been complemented by outright antagonism to genetically engineered crops from antitechnology, antibusiness NGOs [nongovernmental organisations], and some governments, which has caused farmers to become concerned about the acceptability of such crops to importers of seeds and other agricultural products. This is part of the ripple effect of flawed, discriminatory regulation. Finally, the United Nations' brokering of an international agreement on "Liability and Redress" in the event of damages, real or imaginary, from the use of genetically engineered crops is yet another drag on investment in and the use of these products.

What are the implications of this profound and costly policy failure? Mixed, according to Juergen Voegele, director for agriculture and rural development at the World Bank:

> Somewhat higher food prices are a good thing for overall global food production because they stimulate investments in the agricultural sector which are long overdue. Those investments need [to] be economically, socially and environmentally sustainable, everywhere, but particularly in poor countries because they are most vulnerable to climate change and social disruption.

That might be so, but the classic relationship between supply and demand is being distorted by public policy that discourages the private sector investment that would otherwise be stimulated by market forces. Voegele goes on to observe that the inflation of food prices also has negative implications:

> Somewhat higher food prices are a bad thing for the poor because they cannot afford a healthy diet in the first place and are forced to make further cuts on education and health spending if their food bill goes up. We already have close to one billion people go[ing] hungry today, not because there is not enough food in the world but because they cannot afford to buy it.

Regulatory Tragedy

And therein lies the real—and escalating—tragedy of our current, flawed regulatory excesses. Voegele muses about whether we will be able to feed 9 billion people in 2050:

"Food for Fuel," cartoon by John Darkow, *Columbia Daily Tribune*, Missouri, April 16, 2008, www.CagleCartoons.com. Copyright © by John Darkow and www.CagleCartoons.com. All rights reserved.

Without a doubt we can, but not by continuing business as usual. Or we will have 1.5 to 2 billion hungry people in the world by 2050. It will require very significant investments in agriculture R&D and in overall productivity increases.

Greater global food security cannot be accomplished without innovative technology.

But investment alone will not be enough: like trying to run a locomotive with the brakes on, it is wasteful—and ultimately futile—to focus on the "supply side" of research without considering the inhibitory effects of gatekeeper regulation; the regulatory barriers are, in fact, rate limiting.

Greater global food security certainly cannot be accomplished without innovative technology. And that, in turn, cannot be developed in the face of unscientific, gratuitous and excessive regulatory barriers. As Professor Strauss says, "Solving these problems will require new ways of thinking and strong scientific and political leadership to move us toward a regulatory system that enables, rather than arbitrarily blocks, the use of genetic engineering."

He is correct, but there is neither impetus nor momentum to move us in that direction, no hint of bureaucrats' willingness to correct past mistakes. Yet again, the poorest and most vulnerable and powerless among us will suffer most.

GM Will Enslave Farmers and Intensify Hunger

Gathuru Mburu

Gathuru Mburu is director of the Institute for Culture and Ecology based in Thika near Nairobi. In the following viewpoint, he argues that farming practices based on foreign technologies, such as fertilizers, chemical sprays, and genetically modified seeds, are not helpful for Kenya. He says that such techniques damage the land and are unsustainable. Instead, he says, to obtain food security Kenya must turn to local knowledge and communal practices to plant a wide range of indigenous crops. Only in this way, he says, will Kenya be free of foreign control and able to feed all its people.

As you read, consider the following questions:

1. What indigenous fruits and vegetables does Mburu say maize and other exotic crops have replaced?

2. Since what period does Mburu say that Kenya's farmers have been at the mercy of agribusiness, and what does he say caused this?

3. What examples does Mburu provide of ways in which Kenya's food production is not sovereign (that is, not under Kenyan control)?

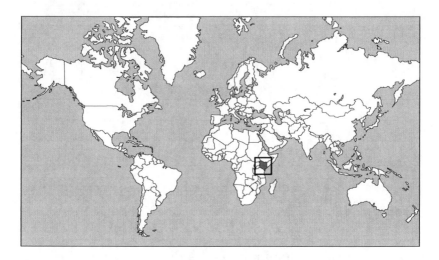

The news of looming hunger in Kenya is worrying. Hunger has now become part of the news, with a section of Kenyan society experiencing it.

In the current situation, many people have rightly or wrongly attributed this situation to post-election violence, but we did not have violence in the previous years, yet people went hungry in many sections of the country.

Recurrent hunger has now become an annual ritual in Kenya, and this is not fair to ourselves as a nation, for we have everything it takes to be sustainably food secure.

This recurrent hunger is of our own making.

We are faced with a more profound problem than we are seeing here. As a nation, we have accepted the global notion that maize security is synonymous with food security, and that when there is no maize there is food insecurity. At the same time, the diversity of indigenous food crops available in Kenya is under threat of extinction because we have made up our minds that anything indigenous is backward.

As farmers, we have space for planting maize and other exotic crops. Tragically, we have little or no space for yams, arrowroots, sweet potatoes, cassava, pumpkins, millet, sorghum and a host of other nutritious indigenous vegetables and fruits.

These crops disappeared a long time ago from our small farms, where we plant maize season in and season out.

As a country, we have failed to take advantage of local biodiversity and the diversity of climatic conditions that support it. We have allowed indigenous flora and fauna to disappear or reduce to near unviable populations as we clear the land for exotic and cash crop farming.

We are in addition faced with an even bigger problem: that of climate change. It is now evident that our country is warming up and seasons are no longer accurately predictable. Our small-scale farming system has been thrown into disarray as it rains when we are expecting a dry spell and vice versa. Farmers are continually being caught unprepared by changing weather patterns.

This recurrent hunger is of our own making.

What is worse, while some indigenous foods are known to be bridging crops that assure food security in times of adverse weather, we are not planting these in sustainable quantities. Maize does not have this capacity and quickly withers when subjected to a short period of water stress.

Our river water volumes are declining with astonishing rapidity, thanks to our equally astonishing zeal to deforest the very water catchment areas that replenish our rivers, and a misguided passion to plant eucalyptus trees, which extract large quantities of water from soils, leaving them dry. In the face of this threat, little if anything is being done to respond to the visible impacts of climate change. We are yet to link climate change to loss of biodiversity and loss of livelihoods.

Until we make this connection and take appropriate action, we will continue facing hunger and will continue begging for food every other year.

Our soils are now dead after being fed with tonnes of chemical fertilisers and sprays for decades. Our farming continues to be dominated by high-external input agriculture, but the farmers do not get enough returns from the same farms to buy these inputs. Our farmers rarely participate in setting prices for their produce while inputs, including seeds, come with fixed prices. It is easy to create demand for farm inputs, but it's difficult to create a demand for farm produce. When it comes to farmers, the law of supply and demand applies to the letter.

This lopsided agribusiness is worsening the hunger situation in Kenya. Honestly, fertilisers and chemical sprays are not the answer to our food problems.

The maize seeds that we rely on so much are graduating from hybrids to genetically modified seeds, which are controlled by multinational companies. Traditionally, the sociology of seeds required that neighbours share seeds within a community. The values of sharing and reciprocity in seed management and food security were essential to ensuring that all members of the community had seeds and food. Yet these values have been trashed by this science of genetic engineering.

Faced with such a threat, our small-scale farmers have a responsibility to rediscover their indigenous foods to secure their families and local economies. There exists a pool of local knowledge about indigenous seeds among local elders. With such a large diversity of communities and seeds in Kenya, we should not be vulnerable to hunger year in year out. We should make our indigenous food biodiversity the benchmark for our food security and our food sovereignty.

Agricultural research in Kenya has fallen. Annual budgetary allocations are dishearteningly minimal. Agricultural research institutions respond to research proposals from whichever source has money irrespective of ethical/legal considerations. Our national agricultural research institution, KARI, has been doing research on genetically modified organisms in the full knowledge that Kenya has no biosafety law, which is a requirement of the Cartagena Protocol on Biosafety.

While trying to remain relevant at an international level, such institutions are increasingly becoming irrelevant nationally. Externally sanctioned research always inclines towards the funders' agenda, at the expense of Kenyan farmers.

The values of sharing and reciprocity ... were essential to ensuring that all members of the community had seeds and food. Yet these values have been trashed by the science of genetic engineering.

Since the 1990s, when Kenya's agricultural extension budget was drastically reduced, farmers have been at the mercy of agribusiness. Farm produce has declined significantly and the soils have been depleted by increased use of chemical fertilisers and sprays. Even when extension services existed, these concentrated more on technical advice than on the social and attitudinal liberation of the farmers' minds.

Kenyans still regard anything exotic as superior to indigenous materials. Our extension services crystallised this self-defeating notion and the trend continues to date, with an over-emphasis on exotic seeds. There is still no talk from government quarters of how farmers can use local knowledge of local biodiversity to improve their livelihoods.

There is minimal research happening on indigenous food biodiversity and our extension officers miss this knowledge. "Scienticising" our indigenous knowledge is the basis for endogenous development, which is what Kenya needs now to liberate our agriculture from the grip of profiteering multinationals.

Food production is now faced with another agribusiness threat called agro-fuels. With global fossil fuel reserves declining at an alarming rate, and on the false premise that agro-fuels will reduce climate change, Kenya is now being wooed into agro-fuel production. Investors are coming in and the government has set up a committee to explore opportunities for Kenya in this newly found, purportedly quick-money and climate ameliorating endeavour.

Huge tracts of virgin land, especially in the drier eastern regions of Kenya, are the target for the diesel-guzzling bull-dozers of agro-fuel investors. Kenya is fast buying into this climate amelioration falsehood, which is transforming cropland into agro-fuel plantations in other countries, reducing farm produce and aggravating the hunger situation. Yet we are all too eager to embrace this hunger-producing investment.

There can be no food sufficiency without food sovereignty.

Since independence, successive governments have failed to lay strong foundations for Kenya's development, whose key pillar is food sufficiency and food sovereignty. Kenyans need enough food produced through a system of production that liberates rather than enslaves them. There can be no food sufficiency without food sovereignty, which is a continuum starting at seed acquisition, planting and management right through to harvesting and post-harvest handling.

Today, our food production is not sovereign at all. There are no options left for farmers who want to grow safe food. Our agriculture has been developed on high external inputs that are not locally available. With prices of these inputs sky-rocketing, Kenya has no option but to explore, sooner rather than later, farmer-friendly, ecological and biodiversity-based farming techniques that provide safe and affordable food.

Until Kenyans have sustained and diversified food reserves at household level, Vision 2030 will remain a mirage.

Kenya and Maize

In Kenya, maize research has been given prominence. It is often said in Kenya that if there is no maize, there is hunger. Consequently, research on most of the traditional crops such as sorghum, millet, roots and tubers (cassava and sweet potatoes) that are drought tolerant have been relegated to the periphery. Though in recent years, KARI [Kenya Agricultural Research Institute] working in close partnership with ICRISAT [International Crops Research Institute for the Semi-Arid Tropics], is conducting research focused on traditional cereals crops—sorghum, millet. Another aspect of food insecurity is linked to post-harvest losses and lack of storage facilities. In the past, homesteads in western Kenya had traditional granary structures for grain storage. Interviews with farmers reveal that these traditional storage structures have collapsed due to low agricultural productivity and food insecurity. Farmers now store grains in gunny bags within the house. At the same time, farmers who grow maize are faced with post-harvest challenges. In 2004, maize farmers lost more than KSh [Kenyan shillings] 7 billion due to attack by a certain stalk borer.

Marie Jocelyn Rarieya,
"Environmental Degradation, Food Security, and Climate Change:
An STS Perspectives on Sustainable Development in Western Kenya,"
Rensselaer Polytechnic Institute, 2007.

At policy level, our seed laws discriminate against community knowledge and ownership of seeds. As a nation, we have perfected the art of legalizing discrimination against communities by recognising individual innovations and knowledge and not what is within the communal realm. Indigenous seeds are communal and the knowledge about them is communally held.

Kenya requires legal tools that recognise and protect this communal phenomenon so that we can support recuperation and sharing of indigenous knowledge of seeds to cushion ourselves from recurrent hunger.

Our leadership must resist being induced into placing our national hopes on maize, genetically modified seeds, fertilisers, chemical sprays and agro-fuels. We must diversify, but in the right manner! We must turn to what is available locally to revitalise our dead soils and use local seeds. We must recognize the space for indigenous knowledge in creating local resilience against the climate challenge.

Our institutions of research and higher learning must be reclaimed to provide the much-needed leadership in research for endogenous development, with support from the government through increased budgetary allocations for research.

Our extension education must be improved to enable extension officers to assist farmers to come down from their delusional comfort zones of "exotic is progress, indigenous is backward". We must strongly hold to what is good of our cultures and improve it through community-led research in conjunction with our research institutions and universities.

We must decolonise our minds, 45 years after political independence, and realise that we have a country to protect. By failing to take charge of our food agenda we are offering ourselves to be re-colonised. For there is no freedom in hunger: We will dance to the tune of those who feed us.

In Australia, Genetically Modified Crops Are Needed to Keep Farming Competitive

Maree McKay

Maree McKay operates a mixed farming enterprise in New South Wales (NSW) and is coordinator of the NSW Producers Forum. In the following viewpoint, she argues that Australia's restrictions on genetically modified (GM) canola has hurt Australian farmers and prevented them from competing in world markets. She says that GM canola has been used for a decade in other countries and is completely safe. She concludes that the government should make it easier for farmers to grow and for researchers to develop GM crops in Australia.

As you read, consider the following questions:

1. What is Australia's biggest export market, and how has Australia's lack of GM canola affected competition in that market, according to McKay?

2. In a long-term trial, how did Jim Pratley find that GM canola outperformed conventional canola varieties?

3. Why does McKay believe that climate change makes GM crops more necessary?

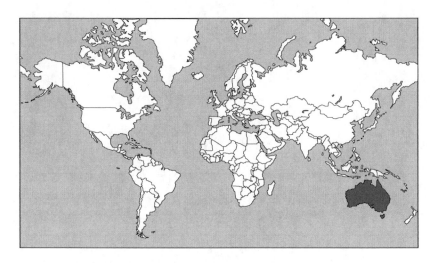

I am one of about 120 farmers from NSW [New South Wales] and Victoria excited to be involved in the small-scale rollout of Australia's first genetically modified (GM) canola varieties [used to produce oils].

GM Canola

Two GM canolas were approved for commercial use by Australia's federal gene technology regulator in 2003 following a rigorous, science-based assessment, but state government bans across the country, based on market issues, have prevented farmers from accessing these new plant varieties until now.

This year [2008], the NSW and Victorian governments lifted their GM canola bans, so a small number of us will finally have the opportunity to grow GM canola and judge its performance for ourselves.

In March, we attended an accreditation course to gather the practical information needed in relation to the agronomic and commercial aspects of the crop, including crop management information, associated costs, monitoring and harvest plans.

Our competitors overseas have had access to GM canola for more than a decade. Canadian farmers have been growing GM canola since 1996 and these varieties now represent around 85 per cent of the country's canola crop. According to a grower survey conducted by the Canola Council of Canada, farmers chose to grow GM canola for easier and better weed control, better yields and reduced costs.

Canada's GM canola is also finding ready markets. Japan is Australia's biggest export market and Japan imports GM canola. More than 85% of canola imported into Japan comes from Canada and is considered to be totally GM. Australian and Canadian canola receives the same price in Japan. There are no significant price premiums for Australian non-GM canola.

Our competitors overseas have had access to GM canola for more than a decade.

According to a long-term trial undertaken by Professor Jim Pratley at Charles Sturt University, which compared the yield and economic performance of a GM herbicide-tolerant canola variety with conventional canola varieties over a typical five-year crop rotation system, the GM canola consistently delivered superior weed control, higher yields and [superior] oil quality when compared to current common canola varieties grown under conventional weed management systems.

Two reports from the University of Melbourne have also predicted positive results from the uptake of GM canola in Australia. They state that the uptake of GM canola would result in an "increase in canola and wheat production worth $135 million to the Australian grains industry," and that the "increased production could be achieved while making the canola industry more sustainable through better integrated weed management and soil conservation practices."

The Australian Bureau of Agricultural and Resource Economics (ABARE) has reported that the potential benefits of GM canola adoption in Australia include yield increases; cheaper and more flexible herbicide use options; reduced costs relating to herbicides, labour, machinery use, and time; environmental and occupational health and safety benefits for on-farm workers; and potential increases in off-farm incomes.

Farmers Need Access to New Technology

For farmers like myself, who rely on new technologies to stay competitive, it has been frustrating waiting to access these new varieties which have been used safely around the world since 1996, especially as all the indications predict positive outcomes.

Whilst this year's GM canola will only represent one to two per cent of the total canola crop, we see this development as a huge step in the right direction. Farmers are business operators who should decide for themselves which varieties suit their enterprises. That said, we understand that some customers may not want to buy GM canola and the grains industry is committed to providing this option.

New agricultural technologies need a predictable research and development process and path to market in order to encourage innovation and investment in Australian agriculture.

New agricultural technologies need a predictable research and development process and path to market in order to encourage innovation and investment in Australian agriculture.

With the effects of climate change dramatically impacting the Australian landscape, farmers like us need Australian researchers to develop new crop varieties, including GM varieties, which are specifically suited to regional conditions. We need access to all the new and emerging tools and technologies available to support our business endeavours.

We hope it has been worth the wait, of course, now it all depends on whether it rains—so we will see what happens.

In India, Genetically Modified Crops Have Caused Economic Disaster

Mae-Wan Ho

Mae-Wan Ho is a British geneticist and the director of the Institute of Science in Society, which advocates against the unethical use of biotechnology. In the following viewpoint, she argues that Indian farmers have gone heavily into debt to buy genetically modified (GM) crops. She says that farmers were promised high crop yields, but instead, the GM crops were vulnerable to drought and to pests. After going heavily into debt to pay for the seeds, farmers experienced low yields and economic ruin, Ho says, and many committed suicide. She blames agribusiness and GM advocates for creating a tragedy in India.

As you read, consider the following questions:

1. According to Ho, what is *lalya*, and what causes it?

2. How many farmers officially committed suicide in India between 1997 and 2007 as stated by Ho, and why does she argue that government records underestimate the total?

3. Whom does Ho single out for what she calls "GM genocide"?

Mae-Wan Ho, "Farmer Suicides and Bt Cotton Nightmare Unfolding in India," Institute of Science in Society, January 6, 2010. Copyright © 2010 by the Institute of Science in Society. All rights reserved. Reproduced by permission.

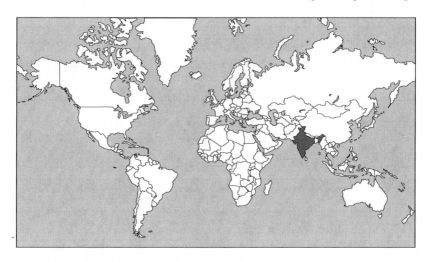

As the cotton-growing season drew to a close in the state of Andhra Pradesh, farmer suicides once again became almost daily occurrences. Officially, the total number of suicides within a six-week period between July and August 2009 stood at 15, but opposition parties and farmers' groups said the true total was more than 150. Opposition leader [Nara] Chandrababu [Naidu] claimed in a speech that he had the names and addresses of 165 farmers who ended their lives because of the distress caused by the drought.

Cotton and Suicide

By November, similar reports were coming from another cotton-growing state Maharashtra. Farmers of Katpur village in Amravati district sowed Bt cotton [a genetically modified crop with pesticide properties] four years ago. Instead of the promised miracle yields, huge debts have driven many to suicide, and cattle were reported dying after feeding on the plants.

One ray of hope was that the 5000-odd farmers of the Maharashtra village have decided to shun Bt cotton, and are now growing soybean instead. Some have also taken to organic farming.

"We were cheated by the seed companies. We did not get the yield promised by them, not even half of it. And the expenditure involved was so high that we incurred huge debts. We have heard that the government is now planning commercial cultivation of Bt brinjal. But we do not want Bt seeds of any crop anymore," said farmer Sahebrao Yawiliker.

Successive studies in Maharashtra have concluded that indebtedness was a major cause of suicides among farmers.

Instead of the promised miracle yields, huge debts have driven many to suicide.

Within a week, two farmers in neighbouring villages in Wardha district killed themselves. Their Bt cotton crops were devastated by *lalya*, a disease that caused the cotton plants to redden and wilt. The first farmer, 55-year-old Laxman Chelpelviar in Mukutban, consumed the pesticide Endosulfan when the first picking from his six-acre farm returned a mere five quintals and an income of Rs15,000 [15,000 rupees], way below his expenses of Rs50,000. The second farmer, 45-year-old Daulat Majure in Jhamkola, was discovered by his mother hanging dead from the ceiling. The cotton yield from his seven-acre farm was a miserable one quintal, worth Rs3,000.

Agricultural scientists said *lalya* points to a lack of micronutrients and moisture content in the soil. *Lalya* develops with pest attacks, moisture stress and lack of micronutrients in the soil. The plant's chlorophyll decreases with nitrogen deficiency, resulting in another pigment, anthocyanin, which turns the foliage red. If reddening starts before boll formation, it results in a 25 percent drop in yield, said a scientist from the Central Institute [for] Cotton Research [CICR] at Nagpur, who wished to remain anonymous. "*Lalya* is here to stay," he declared.

According to the agricultural scientists, the disease has its roots in the American Bt technology that India imported. Almost all of the 500-plus Bt seed varieties sold in India in 2009 are of the same parentage, the American variety Coker312 Bt cotton, a top CICR scientist said. They are F1 hybrids, crossed with Indian varieties.

Coker312 (initially from [the agricultural biotechnology company] Monsanto) showed high susceptibility to attacks by sucking pests like jassids and thrips. The thrips disperse within plant cells, while jassids suck the sap as they multiply under a leaf's surface, forcing the plant to draw more nutrients from the soil, aggravating the soil's nutritional deficiency.

Another characteristic of Bt cotton that depletes the soil is that the bolls come to fruition simultaneously, draining the soil all at once. In a region like Vidarbha, plants wilt in two or three days. "It is like drawing blood from an anemic woman."

A Mismatch Between Crops and Conditions

"If such a technology mismatch continues, soil health and farmers' economy will take a further hit," a top ICAR [Indian Council of Agricultural Research] scientist with years of experience in cotton research was reported saying. "The state needs to take up soil and water conservation efforts on a war footing in Vidarbha."

India has about ten million ha [hectares] under hybrids and Bt cotton, much higher than in China (6.3 m ha), US (3.8 m ha) and Pakistan (3.1 m ha). Unlike India, 79 other countries use self-seeding and non-Bt hybrids.

The cotton crisis and successive crop failures due to declining soil health goes hand in hand with the imported GM (genetic modification) technology, which is energy and input intensive, the report concluded.

Other effects of Bt cotton the Indian scientists could have mentioned are the resurgence of secondary pests and especially the new exotic mealy bug pest introduced with the Bt cotton, as well as the reduced yields of other crops on land cultivated with Bt cotton.

A recent scientific study carried out by Delhi-based Navdanya compared the soil of fields where Bt cotton had been planted for three years with adjoining fields planted with non-GM cotton or other crops. The regions covered included Nagpur, Amravati and Wardha of Vidarbha, which account for the highest Bt cotton planting in India, and the highest rate of farmer suicides (4,000 per year).

In three years, Bt cotton was found to reduce the population of actinomycetes bacteria by 17 percent. Actinomycetes bacteria are vital for breaking down cellulose and creating humus [organic matter from decayed plants that helps fertilise soil].

A decade of planting with GM cotton . . . could lead to total destruction of soil organisms, "leaving dead soil unable to produce food."

Bacteria overall were reduced by 14 percent, while the total microbial biomass was reduced by 8.9 percent. Vital soil enzymes, which make nutrients available to plants, have also been drastically reduced. Acid phosphatase, which contributes to the uptake of phosphates, was lowered by 26.6 percent. Nitrogenase enzymes, which help fix nitrogen [that is, turn nitrogen into compounds important for plants], were diminished by 22.6 percent. The study concluded that a decade of planting with GM cotton, or any GM crop with Bt genes, could lead to total destruction of soil organisms, "leaving dead soil unable to produce food."

After some respite in the post-loan-waiver year of 2008, farmer suicides have begun to climb again. The number of suicides in the six worst-affected western Vidarbha districts in 2009 was approaching 900. November saw 24 farmers take their own lives in Yavatmal alone.

"Crop survival this year is only 44 percent in some blocks," said Sanjay Desmukh, Yavatmal collector. "Rains have been scanty."

Indebtedness and the Deadly Consequences

According to Indian government records, 182,936 farmers committed suicide in India between 1997 and 2007. Nearly two-thirds occurred in five states, Maharashtra, Karnataka, Andhra Pradesh, Madhya Pradesh and Chhattisgarh, with one-third of the country's population. The count has been rising even as the numbers of farmers are diminishing. As many as 8 million quit farming between 1991 and 2001, and the rate of quitting has only risen since.

These official figures tend to be huge underestimates. The records are collated by the National Crime Records Bureau, a wing of the Ministry of Home Affairs, but the numbers reported to the bureau by the states are often massaged downwards. For example, women farmers are not normally accepted as farmers, as by custom, land is never in their names, although they do the bulk of the work in agriculture.

P. Sainath, the rural affairs editor of the *Hindu* and author of *Everybody Loves a Good Drought,* refers to the suicides as "the largest sustained wave of such deaths recorded in history," and attributes it to India's "embrace of the brave new world of neoliberalism."

The rate of farmers' suicides has worsened particularly after 2002 (the year GM crops were introduced to India, although Sainath does not say so). Between 1997 and 2001, the number of suicides was 78,737, or 15,747 a year on average. Between 2002 and 2006, the number was 87,567, or 17,513 a year on average.

Those who have taken their lives were deep in debt (as successive studies in Maharashtra confirmed). Peasant households in debt nearly doubled in the first decade of the neoliberal[1] "economic reforms," from 26 percent of farm households to 48.6 percent, according to the National Sample Survey [Office] data. But in the worst affected states, the rate of indebtedness is far higher. For example, 82 percent of all farm households in Andhra Pradesh were in debt by 2001–02.

Furthermore, those who killed themselves were overwhelmingly cash crop farmers growing cotton, coffee, sugarcane, groundnut, pepper and vanilla. Suicides were fewer among those that grow food crops such as rice, wheat, maize and pulses.

Giant seed companies have been displacing cheap hybrids and far cheaper and hardier traditional varieties with their own products. A cotton farmer buying Monsanto's GM cotton would be paying far more for seed. Local varieties and hybrids were squeezed out with enthusiastic state support.

In 1991, farmers could buy a kilogram of local seed for as little as Rs7 or Rs9 in today's worst affected region of Vidarbha. By 2003, they would pay Rs350 (US$7) for a 450-gram bag of hybrid seed. By 2004, Monsanto's partners in India were marketing a 450-gram bag of Bt cotton seed for between Rs1,650 and Rs1,800 ($33 to $36). This price was brought down by government intervention overnight in Andhra Pradesh, where the government changed after the 2004 elections. The price dropped to around Rs900 ($18), still many times higher than 1991 or even 2003.

Health and food costs skyrocketed while farmers' incomes crashed, and so did the price they got for their cash crops, thanks to subsidies to corporate and rich farmers in the US

---

1. Neoliberalism is an approach to development that stresses market-based solutions and open trade.

and EU [European Union]. These subsidies on cotton alone destroyed cotton farmers not only in India but in African nations such as Burkina Faso, Benin, Mali and Chad.

As costs rose, credit dried up and debt went out of control, and the tides of suicides washed over India.

But there is yet a more "sinister reason" for the mass suicides: GM crops, notably BT cotton.

To add to the farmers' plight, the unsustainable farming practices are coming home to roost. More than 1,500 farmers in the state of Chhattisgarh committed suicide, driven into debt by crop failures due to falling water levels, which dropped from 40 feet to below 250 feet in just the past few years.

But there is yet a more "sinister reason" for the mass suicides: GM crops, notably Bt cotton. Millions of Indian farmers had been promised undreamt of harvests by switching to planting GM seeds. They borrowed money to buy the exorbitant seeds, only to find their crops failing miserably, leaving them with spiraling debt from which the only exit is suicide. British journalist Andrew Malone writing for the *Daily Mail* reported an estimated 125,000 farmers had taken their own lives directly as the result of GM crops; the crisis being branded "GM genocide" by campaigners. It is perpetrated by powerful GM lobbyists and prominent politicians all over the world who persist in claiming that GM crops have transformed Indian agriculture and are producing greater yields than ever before.

Malone described how he travelled to Maharashtra in the suicide belt to find out for himself who is telling the truth. There he witnessed the cremation of the body of the farmer in a cracked, barren field near his home 100 miles from Nagpur in central India.

Bt Cotton Around the World

Bt cotton is a cotton variety that has been genetically engineered for resistance to some of its key insect pests. The pros and cons of Bt cotton are one of the most hotly debated subjects around the world. The biotech industry has made unprecedented claims and promises about Bt cotton, extensively advertising and promoting the benefits of such genetically modified organisms (GMOs) for farmers and the environment. However, the experience of Bt cotton farmers in many countries of the Global South completely contradicts the claims of the industry.

Makhathini region in South Africa has been showcased by Monsanto as the grand success of Bt cotton for small farmers. In reality, today Makhathini groans under the burden of Bt cotton which has totally failed its small farmers. Indonesia kicked out Bt cotton just one year after it began to be grown by farmers in Sulawesi. In Thailand, Bt cotton has been cunningly promoted by the biotech industry by subverting national laws. In India, the industry touted Bt cotton as the panacea for cotton farmers' misery. But within five years of being introduced, Bt cotton cultivation has generated a deep crisis and death among farming communities. In order to avoid a similar fate, a citizens' jury in Mali (West Africa) that included different types of farmers rejected Bt cotton's entry into their country. The farmers' jury issued a stiff warning to the Malian government, demanding that no genetically engineered crops be allowed into Mali.

P.V. Satheesh and Michel Pimbert,
Affirming Life and Diversity:
Rural Images and Voices on Food Sovereignty
in South India. London: International Institute
for Environment and Development, 2008.

Death by Insecticide

"As flames consumed the corpse, Ganjanan, 12, and Kalpana, 14, faced a grim future. While Shankara Mandauka had hoped his son and daughter would have a better life under India's economic boom, they now face working as slave labour for a few pence a day. Landless and homeless, they will be the lowest of the low," Malone wrote.

Shankara drank insecticide to end his life 24 hours earlier. He was in debt for two years' earnings and could see no other way out of his despair.

"There were still marks in the dust where he had writhed in agony. Other villagers looked on—they knew from experience that any intervention was pointless—as he lay doubled up on the ground, crying out in pain and vomiting."

Neighbours gathered to pray outside the family home. Nirmala Mandaukar told how she rushed back from the fields to find her husband dead. "He was a loving and caring man," she said, weeping.

Shankara's crop, Bt cotton, had failed twice. Like millions of other Indian farmers, he switched from traditional seeds to GM seeds, beguiled by the promise of bumper harvests and future riches. He borrowed money to buy the GM seeds. But when the harvests failed, he was left with mounting debts and no income.

"Simple, rural people, they are dying slow, agonizing deaths. Most swallow insecticide—a pricey substance they were promised they would not need when they were coerced into growing expensive GM crops," Malone wrote. "Pro-GM experts claim that it is rural poverty, alcoholism, drought and 'agrarian distress' that is the real reason for the horrific toll. But as I discovered during a four-day journey through the epicentre of the disaster, that is not the full story."

In one village, he found 18 farmers had committed suicide after being "sucked" into GM debt. Village after village, families told how they had fallen into debt on being persuaded to buy GM seeds. Famers paid £10 for 100 g [grams] of GM seeds, a thousand times the cost of traditional seeds. The GM salesmen and government officials promised farmers that these were "magic seeds" that yield better crops without parasites and insects.

Far from being magic seeds, the GM crops were devastated by bollworms. They also required double the amount of water.

When rains failed for the past two years, many GM crops simply withered and died.

In the past when crops failed, farmers could still save seeds and replant them the following year. But with GM hybrid seeds, they have been unable to do that.

When rains failed for the past two years, many GM crops simply withered and died.

Suresh Bhalasa was another farmer cremated the same week, leaving a wife and two children. His family had no doubt that their troubles began the moment they were encouraged to buy Monsanto's Bt cotton.

"We are ruined now," said the 38-year-old widow. "We bought 100 grams of Bt cotton. Our crop failed twice. My husband had become depressed. He went out to the field, lay down in the cotton and swallowed insecticide."

China Must Develop Genetically Modified Crops to Mitigate Climate Change

Lan Lan

Lan Lan is a business reporter at China Daily. *In the following viewpoint, she reports that Chinese scientists and officials believe that genetically modified (GM) crops may help mitigate the effects of climate change. GM crops can resist drought and produce high crop yields, Lan Lan says. She reports that China already imports GM crops. However, the government wants to encourage the development of China's own GM strains in order to reduce reliance on foreign technology. Lan Lan reports that while environmental groups are wary of GM crops, many scientists feel there is relatively little risk to using them and possibly great benefits.*

As you read, consider the following questions:

1. Lan Lan discusses at length one GM crop that China imports. What is the crop, and from where does China import it?

2. What did Monsanto do to make its seeds more adaptable to China's situation, according to Lan Lan?

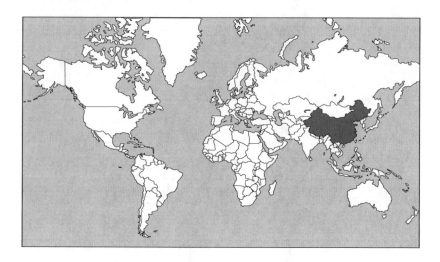

3. What evidence does Ajit Maru provide that the world is not short of food?

The Chinese consume millions of tons of genetically modified (GM) soybean oil every year without fuss despite the fact that attitudes toward GM food remain as divergent in the nation as they are in the rest of the world.

More Innovation Is Needed

China needs to step up agricultural innovation, including development of its own GM varieties, in response to climate change and to reduce reliance on foreign technologies, top agricultural experts and scientists told *China Business Weekly* last week [August 2010].

The genetic modification of food involves the insertion of genes from one variety of a crop to another in order to transfer certain desired characteristics such as insect resistance or drought tolerance.

The technology is controversial. Critics say it is inherently risky to mess with nature. Supporters say it will prevent food shortages.

GM crops can provide solutions to various problems facing the ecosystem such as limited land and water resources, scientists say.

"Making technical preparations for transgenic technology is very necessary for China," said Zhai Huqu, president of the Chinese Academy of Agricultural Sciences.

GM crops can provide solutions to various problems facing the ecosystem such as limited land and water resources, scientists say.

However, the government has yet to approve use of the technology, Zhai said.

Last year, China issued biosafety certificates to two strains of pest-resistant GM rice and corn. The strains still need about three to five years of registration and production trials before commercialization.

"Apart from transgenic soybean oil there should not be any GM crops on the market," Zhai said.

China has been a net importer of soybeans since the mid-1990s. Imported soybeans from the United States and Argentina are mainly genetically modified.

China consumes about 10 million tons of soybean oil and about 40 million tons of soybean meal per year in processed food and animal feedstuff, industry analysts said.

More than 80 percent of the total is imported GM soybean oil or made from imported GM soybeans.

Approval has not been given for the import of GM crop seeds.

China and Monsanto

International companies such as Monsanto, which have already sold seeds of GM cotton and conventional crops in China, have started exploring the potential GM market in China.

53

The majority of US and Argentina corn producers have adopted GM technologies, said Kevin Eblen, Monsanto's regional leader in North Asia and president of Monsanto China.

"We are working to get those approvals in China," he said.

To make its seeds more adaptable to China's situation, the company set up a research and development center in China last December and carried out joint research with several Chinese institutes.

"We are here in China to try to find the best products for China's soil type, climate and environmental conditions," said Eblen.

He declined to reveal Monsanto's revenue or market share in China. The published annual global revenue of the company is roughly $11 billion.

China is the number one growth opportunity for Monsanto in the long term, he said.

"China for us today is still a relatively small piece of our overall business but, obviously, with the size of agriculture here, particularly in crops that we are involved in, such as corn, vegetables and cotton, there are opportunities for our business here," he said.

Companies including Monsanto have developed crops with high drought tolerance.

Chinese agricultural research institutes should catch up and develop their own anti-drought crops to reduce possible reliance on foreign technologies, said scientists.

"Currently we only deal with disasters such as droughts or floods passively when they occur, which isn't a long-term solution," said Wang Ren, director of the Consultative Group on International Agricultural Research.

As climate change is bringing more uncertainties, it's urgent for China to move quickly to develop its own anti-drought varieties, both conventional and GM products, he said.

To ensure China's food security, the key is to enhance its agricultural technology level in all aspects, Wang said.

"GM is a potential technology, but its development must be well under the nation's transgenic safety and quality assessment system. All things should be assessed under the framework," he warned.

The nation needs to carefully study what kind of products will be needed in the next 15 years when investing in agricultural technologies, said Shenggen Fan, director general of the Washington [DC]-based International Food Policy Research Institute.

Factors such as climate change and alterations to water resources need to be taken into consideration when designing the plans, he said.

As climate change is bringing more uncertainties, it's urgent for China to move quickly to develop its own anti-drought varieties.

The Risks Are Low

Environmental groups such as Greenpeace have long expressed concerns about the spread of GM food. Disputes over GM food are most intense in Japan and Europe.

In February, the Indian government reversed a decision to allow Monsanto to sell its GM eggplant crop in India. The decision to commercialize the eggplant sparked concerns that the market might be monopolized and the product could threaten the health of humans.

Fan said GM technology provides a new choice. It's good for increasing the income of farmers and reducing costs to consumers. However, at the same time, new technologies always have risks.

Scientists should provide statistics and reports about any impact on health and the environment. It must be the farmers

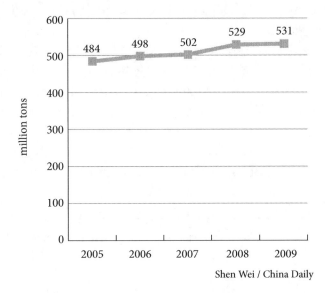

Grain Production in China

China's grain production has increased, but the government hopes GM technology may spark even greater growth.

Shen Wei / China Daily

TAKEN FROM: Lan Lan, "China Told to Develop Its Own GM Food," *China Daily*, August 23, 2010. www.chinadaily.com.cn.

and consumers who make the final decision whether or not to plant or consume GM food, said experts.

Fan urged the government to take environmental protection into consideration in transgenic technology development from the very beginning.

Anton Mangstl, director of the Office of Knowledge Exchanges Research and Extension of Food and Agriculture Organization of the United Nations, said GM technology was one direction for agriculture.

"If the technology can be used in a wise way, I personally believe GM technology in the long term can be a contribution to agricultural food security," he said.

The high-level tolerance of some GM plants can address various problems that the ecosystem is facing from such things as drought and insects, said 2004 World Food Prize Laureate Monty Jones, executive director of Forum for Agricultural Research in Africa.

"So far there are no major problems to health. I agree there might be problems that have yet to be identified, but the risks are very, very low," he said.

The high-level tolerance of some GM plants can address various problems that the ecosystem is facing from such things as drought and insects.

People for and against GM food should stop fighting and come together, do surveys from time to time, every year or every two years, look at the potential and the benefits and the risks, if there are any, so they are able to advise the community, he added.

"When you don't know something, how do you judge it? You can't and shouldn't stop science, but choices should be made by society. We can control it," said Ajit Maru of the Global Forum on Agricultural Research.

About 40 percent of the food in the world is wasted in various ways, either in losses or not eaten. The globe is not short of food in that sense, but short of being able to use food effectively, he added.

Genetically Engineered Crops Will Not Help Mitigate Climate Change

Pete Riley, Kirtana Chandrasekaran, and Ronnie Hall

Pete Riley, Kirtana Chandrasekaran, and Ronnie Hall are all activists and writers with Friends of the Earth International. In the following viewpoint, they argue that there is little evidence that genetically modified (GM) crops will provide higher yields in drought or stress conditions caused by global warming. Nor, they argue, is there much evidence that growing GM crops can reduce carbon emissions through efficient land use or the creation of new biofuels. Instead, they say, GM crops are a distraction from finding real solutions to climate change such as those provided by agroecology and organic farming methods.

As you read, consider the following questions:

1. What do the authors say intensive crop and livestock farming methods require?
2. According to the authors, what four crops is GM production largely confined to, and what six countries make up the vast bulk of the area in which they are grown?

3. What problems result when private companies patent genetic resources, according to the authors?

Even though claims that genetically modified (GM) crops can solve hunger and poverty remain unproven, a new claim has recently emerged: that GM crops will be one of the solutions to combating climate change.

This claim is based on a range of arguments, including a rehashing of older declarations that GM crops reduce pesticide use and increase yields, meaning that they will be useful in both mitigating and adapting to climate change. An additional new argument is that GM crops will reduce the loss of carbon from soil by reducing tillage. It is also being claimed that new drought-resistance crops are about to be commercialized. Biotech companies are lobbying hard at the UN's [United Nations'] climate change negotiations, for GM crops and industrial farming methods, which are responsible for up to 50% of global emissions of nitrous oxide, to be recognized as mitigation techniques in agriculture.

As a result, governments and private funders such as the [Bill and Melinda] Gates Foundation are ramping up their investments in GM research. In the UK [United Kingdom], for example, the government spent £49 million on biotechnology in 2006/2007, compared to just £1.6 million on organic farming. In October 2009, the Gates Foundation announced a further US$120 million grant for agriculture in Africa. At the press launch Bill Gates [head of the Gates Foundation] said, "Biotechnology has a critical role to play in increasing agricultural productivity, particularly in light of climate change."

The Solution Is Not More of the Same

GM crops have been developed as part of the intensive model of agriculture that has dominated farming over the last 60 years. Intensive crop and livestock farming methods require large inputs of oil, artificial fertilizers, pesticides and the use of hybrid seeds. Collectively these are major contributors to climate change, since they lead to increases in greenhouse gas emissions, reductions in soil carbon, soil erosion and habitat destruction. The International Assessment of Agricultural Knowledge, Science and Technology for Development (IAASTD), which has an intergovernmental governance structure, has concluded that "business as usual is not an option" and that farming practices will have to change radically to meet the challenges of climate change. These will include feeding a growing population, protecting and restoring biodiversity and ecosystems services, and producing fuel and raw materials for industry.

The model of GM farming, like other forms of intensive agriculture, is reliant on highly expensive technology and energy-intensive inputs.

The GM industry has also failed to gain acceptance for GM plant varieties as food crops in important markets especially in Europe, Africa, Japan and, most recently, India. This is primarily due to public and political concern about the potential socioeconomic, environmental and health impacts of GM crops.

Many of the industry's claims about GM technology turn out to be exaggerations or entirely premature. In addition, the model of GM farming, like other forms of intensive agriculture, is reliant on highly expensive technology and energy-intensive inputs. To rely on such uncertain claims would be very foolish given the urgent need to tackle the causes and effects of climate change.

GM is a false solution to climate change. It is also highly expensive to develop and thus suppresses the development of other approaches. Meanwhile the value of local agricultural knowledge and agroecology continues to be recognized in recent reports. But, agroecological alternatives receive little attention and even less funding from governments and private charities such as that of Bill Gates, when compared to investments in GM and biotechnology.

Examining the Evidence on GM Farming and Climate Change

Claim #1: GM farming increases carbon retention in soils. "Soil carbon" refers to the organic matter present in most soils, which can be released as carbon dioxide if soils are disturbed; such disturbances are common in industrial agriculture and logging, and contribute to climate change. A technique known as "conservation tillage", which leaves some of the crop residues or stubble on the surface rather than plowing it back into the ground, is used to minimize the disturbance of the soil and soil erosion.

The claim that GM technology can increase the relative retention of carbon stored in soil comes from the use of such zero or minimum tillage cultivation techniques with GM crops. However, "conservation tillage" was developed well before the first GM crops appeared and is in no way specific to GM crops. It was originally intended to enhance soil and water conservation.

Furthermore, the introduction of GM herbicide tolerant crops (GMHT) is undermining the sustainability of these earlier conservation tillage systems, by increasing the quantity of herbicides used and because of soil compaction by repeated use of heavy machinery, for example in the central Pampas region of [South America]. Indeed some reports suggest that a reduction in overall emissions of greenhouse gases from zero-tillage systems is not proven because of increased carbon dioxide and nitrous oxide emissions. In addition, recent studies suggest that "no-till", one particular form of conservation tillage, has environmental benefits such as reducing soil erosion, but may not sequester more carbon than conventional tillage (plowing).

Importantly, the overall claim is also based on the promise that GM herbicide-tolerant crops will lead to a reduction in the quantity of herbicide applied because of the use of just one herbicide, the elimination of pre-sowing applications of herbicides, and fewer applications on the growing crop. However, after more than a decade cultivating GMHT in North and South America, evidence from both governmental agencies and academics confirms that the crops actually increase herbicide use. A recent review found that in the 13 years since GMHT crops were introduced in the US, the amount of herbicide applied had increased by around 144,000 tonnes.

It is also notable that the claims made about GM crops' relative ability to sequester carbon in soil are based on comparisons with other forms of intensive agricultural production. They tend to overlook agricultural practices based on agroecological principles in which carbon-rich materials, such as manure and compost, are systematically returned to the soil to improve it. There are also other types of conservation tillage, including methods suitable for organic farming systems, in which the use of chemical herbicides is not permitted....

Claim #2: GM crops reduce greenhouse gas emissions from farm operations. This claim is based on the idea that herbicide tolerant GM crops require fewer herbicide applications, thus saving fuel by reducing the number of tractor passes across the field. This claim is closely connected to that of zero tillage as the two systems go hand in hand. These promises initially encouraged farmers to buy GMHT seeds: They expected improved weed control and reduced fuel and labor costs. However, after a brief "honeymoon period" when GMHT crops were first introduced in 1996, problems began to emerge....

In the US, Argentina and Brazil, where the majority of GMHT crops are grown, the promise of reduced herbicide use has been seriously undermined by the development of weeds with strong resistance to herbicides such as Roundup. This means other or additional chemical herbicides have to be used....

The impact of resistance is also being felt in the US where an analysis of pesticide usage based on official data showed that GM crops have actually resulted in a net increase in pesticide use—compared with pre-GM figures, an additional 0.11kg [kilograms] of pesticide was applied per acre in 2008. GM crops are generally pushing pesticide use upward in the US. In 2008, for example, GM crop acres required over 26% more pesticide per acre in the US than conventional varieties. This trend is projected to continue. . . .

Claims that GMHT crops would lead to lower labor costs . . . and that they are climate friendly . . . are increasingly found to be wanting.

In conclusion, claims that GMHT crops would lead to lower labor costs and reduced herbicide applications, and that they are climate friendly because of reduced tillage, are increasingly found to be wanting. . . .

GM Crops and Hunger

Claim #3: GM crops will feed us in a warming world. It is frequently claimed that GM crops produce higher yields than conventional crops, meaning that more food should be produced from the same area of land. The argument is that this would alleviate the need for increased land for agriculture, which currently leads to the destruction of forests and other carbon-rich ecosystems. But none of the GM crops so far developed for commercial cultivation has been yield enhancing, and there is no evidence to support this claim. Rather than increasing yield, the focus has been on agronomic traits and over 99% of commercial GM crops are modified to create herbicide tolerance or insect resistance (or both).

The largest and most comprehensive assessment of agricultural science, the International Assessment of Agricultural Knowledge, Science and Technology for Development

(IAASTD) examined the evidence for GM and found no definite evidence that GM crops were yield enhancing. . . .

Yield is a complex phenomenon that depends on numerous factors, including weather, the availability of irrigation and fertilizers, soil quality, farmers' management skills, and levels of pest infestation. Genetic improvements achieved through conventional (i.e., non-biotechnological) breeding are also important. Indeed, traditional plant breeding has continued since GM crops were first introduced and hence the steady rise in overall yields since 1996 can be attributed to this general trend, which started in the 1930s.

A recently published review [by the Union of Concerned Scientists], which closely evaluated the overall effect that genetic engineering has had on crop yields in relation to other agricultural technologies, observes that GM technology has had little or no overall impacts on crop yields:

> Overall, corn and soybean yields have risen substantially over the last 15 years, but largely not as a result of the GE [genetically engineered] traits. Most of the gains are due to traditional breeding or improvement of other agricultural practices. . . .

The overall contribution of GM crops to global food supply remains small in comparison to other crops bred in a conventional manner. There is no commercial production of most of the world's staple crops—wheat, barley, oats, potatoes, rice, sorghum, cassava, and millet (although in 2009, China did grant safety certificates for small-scale field trials of GM rice and GM maize). With the exceptions of small areas of papaya and squashes in the USA and tomatoes and sweet peppers in China, no GM fruit and vegetables have been developed to the point of commercial cultivation either.

GM production is largely confined to four crops: soya, maize, oilseed rape and cotton are grown on over 99% of the total area under GM cultivation. And 95% of the area grown is in just six countries: the US, Brazil, Argentina, Canada, China and India. In 2009 industry sources reported that 134 million ha [hectares] of GM crops were being grown in the world: This amounts to just 2.7% of farmed land. The proportion of the world's farmers actively growing GM crops—14 million according to the industry—is around 1.1% of the total 1.3 billion farmers. It is important that the claims being made for GM crops' ability to contribute to alleviating the impacts of climate change–induced hunger are assessed in the light of this data.

The overall contribution of GM crops to global food supply remains small in comparison to other crops bred in a conventional manner.

In addition, between 66% and 90% of all soya production is fed to animals, mainly in very inefficient intensive production systems (the ratio of plant protein needed to produce one unit of animal protein varies between 5 and 9 depending on the system being employed). The GM crop industry is thus contributing directly to industrial livestock production, which is also a major producer of greenhouse gases through land clearance (6%) and methane emissions (6%). . . .

GM Crops, Drought and Biofuels

Claim #4: "Miracle" new GM crops will produce food during drought and stress. There is much made of "miracle" GM crops, that would be capable of growing in "marginal lands" or dealing with environmental extremes. Crops might, for example, be modified to cope with abiotic stresses such as salinity, high levels of aluminum in soils or drought. But these crops are nowhere near commercial cultivation at the moment. . . .

Genetic engineers have been trying to convert plants so that they make more efficient use of carbon dioxide and water. . . . Successful genetic modification conferring drought tolerance has so far proved impossible because this requires major changes to the metabolism of the plant. It is also worth pointing out that no seed will germinate and flourish in the absence of any moisture, which is so often the case in prolonged periods of drought in Africa, Australia and Europe. . . .

In contrast, traditional breeding has produced varieties that mature quickly, increasing the chances of achieving a harvestable crop in some dry years. In other words, solutions already exist or are seriously viable, and it is these that need to be further researched in the interest of mitigating the impacts of climate change. . . .

Successful genetic modification conferring drought tolerance has so far proved impossible because this requires major changes to the metabolism of the plant.

Claim #5: Crops can be genetically modified to provide fuels. A member of the European biofuels industry commented that,

> In many ways, genetically modified (GM) crops and biofuels are made for each other. The enhanced yields available from the current generation of GM crops such as corn and soybeans can help farmers meet the growing feedstock demand for biofuels while still producing sufficient quantities of food and animal feed. In the future, GM crops with even higher yields and entirely novel GM varieties of grasses and trees should make biofuels production even more efficient and inexpensive.

In reality, however, the potential to increase yields from GM crops to supply demand for agrofuel feedstocks is far from proven. . . . This would require genetic changes that would fundamentally alter the metabolism of the plant and there is no certainty that the resulting plant will be able to thrive in the environment and produce high yields because successful crop plants are the sum of genetics, interaction between different genes, and interaction between genes and the environment. Introducing or changing a gene is thus no guarantee of success. Agrofuels production is also constrained by the limited efficiency of photosynthesis in converting solar energy into biomass (in practice only about 3–6% of total solar radiation is converted into biomass); and by the availability of productive land that is not being used for other purposes. . . .

The claims about the role of GM crops and trees in replacing fossil fuels is based on very limited evidence and poor analysis of the environmental and socioeconomic impacts that such a major shift in land use would have. . . . Several detailed critiques have also been published exposing the threat of uncontrolled expansion of agrofuel production in general which could lead to:

- Loss of land previously used for food production

- Displacement of farmers and indigenous peoples

- Damage to biodiversity

- Increased agrochemical use (pesticides and fertilizers) and pollution from intensively managed plantations

- Poor working conditions

- Human rights abuses, and

- Substantial increases in GHG [greenhouse gas] emissions. . . .

Genetic Modification Threatens Real Solutions to Climate Change

Patents are used by large transnational corporations to protect markets and prevent farmers from saving seeds from crops to sow the next year. The enforcement of such patents has been applied to control farming and ensure that biotechnology companies retain seed sales. The same companies (Monsanto,

Bayer [CropScience], Syngenta [AG], BASF and DuPont) are systematically patenting any natural genes which could at some point be included in crops modified to mitigate and adapt to the changing conditions associated with climate change: drought, salinity, floods, high and low temperatures, and other abiotic stresses, as well as chemical loads in water and general stress. So far they have filed 532 patent documents covering 55 patent families.

The privatization of genetic resources in this way restricts farmers' and researchers' access to seeds and knowledge, and fuels the development of powerful monopolies. The top ten seed companies in the world already control 57% of seed sales. But restricting farmers' access to seeds, which they traditionally rely on from one year to the next by saving seeds from each crop, is a threat to their food sovereignty.

In Africa there is also growing concern that the patenting of climate genes will undermine local initiatives for dealing with the huge challenge of climate change[. According to the African Centre for Biosafety]:

> Patent monopolies undermine and stymie climate adaptation by African farmers because it constrains the free exchange of and experimentation with crop germplasm—critical activities for the development of African solutions. . . .

Genetically modifying crops to allow agriculture to adapt to and mitigate climate change is a high-risk strategy. Few of the supposed "savior" crops have actually been demonstrated to work in the field, and their ability to meet much-publicized expectations remains unknown. None have yet been commercialized. Davinder Sharma, an Indian commentator on agriculture and GM crops, succinctly sums up why such claims are being made:

> These assertions are not amusing, and can no longer be taken lightly. I am not only shocked but also disgusted at the way corporations try to fabricate and distort the scien-

tific facts, and dress them up in such a manner that the so-called "educated" of today will accept them without asking any questions.

This focus on GM technology diverts attention away from another successful approach to agriculture that already has a proven track record when it comes to addressing some of the challenges linked to climate change: agroecology. This system of food production is championed by Via Campesina, the global network of peasant farmers, who observe that:

> Agroecology and other sustainable food production systems are preserving biodiversity and increasing food productivity. These systems have in practice shown alternatives to the high-tech, expensive and unsustainable model of the "green revolution."

This focus on GM technology diverts attention away from another successful approach to agriculture . . . agroecology.

In April 2008, the International Assessment of Agricultural Knowledge, Science and Technology for Development (IAASTD) published its report based on four years of deliberation looking into the scientific, social science and economic aspects of the genetic modification of crops. The report included 20 key findings, amongst which was a call for far greater emphasis on agroecological approaches to land management and the need to develop agricultural knowledge, science and technology (AKST) to this end.

> An increase and strengthening of AKST towards agroecological sciences will contribute to addressing environmental issues while maintaining and increasing productivity. Formal, traditional and community-based AKST needs to respond to increasing pressures on natural resources, such as reduced availability and worsening quality of water, de-

graded soils and landscapes, loss of biodiversity and agro-ecosystem function, degradation and loss of forest cover and degraded marine and inshore fisheries.

The overriding message of the report was summed up thus [by Professor Robert Watson, director IAASTD and chief scientist for the UK's Department for Environment, Food and Rural Affairs]:

> Agriculture has a footprint on all of the big environmental issues, so as the world considers climate change, biodiversity, land degradation, water quality, etc., they must also consider agriculture which lies at the centre of these issues and poses some uncomfortable challenges that need to be faced. We've got to make sure the footprint of agriculture on climate change is lessened; we have to make sure that we don't degrade our soil, we don't degrade the water, and we don't have adverse effects on biodiversity. There are some major challenges, but we believe that by combining local and traditional knowledge with formal knowledge these challenges can be met.

The IAASTD did not endorse GM crops as the solution, much to the annoyance of the biotechnology industry and the USA, Australia and Canada, all of whom provided amended text to the final report to record their disquiet. However, 58 counties have endorsed the IAASTD findings without such reservations.

Periodical and Internet Sources Bibliography

The following articles have been selected to supplement the diverse views presented in this chapter.

Rajesh Chhabara	"Climate Ready GM Crops: The Patent Race," ClimateChangeCorp, September 17, 2008. www.climatechangecorp.com.
Laurie Goering	"Relying on GM Crops to Battle Climate Change 'Suicidal,' Indian Activist Charges," Common Dreams, March 15, 2010. www.commondreams.org.
Ethan A. Huff	"Monsanto Connected to at Least 200,000 Suicides in India Throughout Past Decade," Natural News, January 4, 2011. www.naturalnews.com.
Robert Langreth and Matthew Herper	"The Planet Versus Monsanto," *Forbes*, January 18, 2010.
Jessica Marshall	"Can GM Plants Combat Climate Change?," Discovery News, December 29, 2010. http://news.discovery.com.
Kumi Naidoo	"Australia's GM Wheat Will Only Worsen World Hunger," Drum Opinion, July 5, 2011. www.abc.net.au.
John Robbins	"Can GMOs Help End World Hunger?," *Huffington Post*, August 1, 2011. www.huffingtonpost.com.
Rachel Shields	"GM Crops Have a Role in Preventing World Hunger, Chief Scientist Says," *Independent* (UK), November 19, 2009.
World Health Organization	"20 Questions on Genetically Modified Foods," 2012. www.who.int.

GLOBALVIEWPOINTS

CHAPTER 2

Genetic Engineering and Disease

In Germany and the United States, Bee Colony Crashes May Be Linked to Genetically Modified Crops

Gunther Latsch

Gunther Latsch is a journalist at the German newspaper Der Spiegel. *In the following viewpoint, he reports that bee populations are falling in Germany. He says the situation is even worse in the United States, where colonies are collapsing at unprecedented rates. Latsch notes that bees are vital for pollination and that a disappearance of bees would have a serious effect on human life. He reports that there is some evidence that the collapse of colonies may be linked to the growing use of genetically modified (GM) crops.*

As you read, consider the following questions:

1. Besides GM crops, what other causes may be reducing bee populations in Germany, according to the viewpoint?

2. How much value do bees generate, and through what activities, according to researchers at Cornell University?

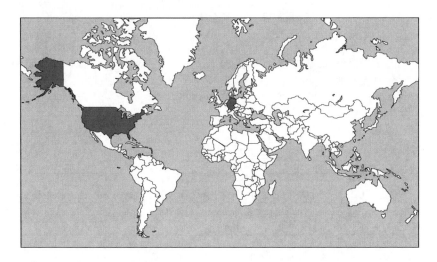

3. What signs does Latsch report that suggest that bee immune systems were affected in colony collapse disorder?

A mysterious decimation of bee populations has German beekeepers worried, while a similar phenomenon in the United States is gradually assuming catastrophic proportions. The consequences for agriculture and the economy could be enormous.

Disappearing Bees

Walter Haefeker is a man who is used to painting grim scenarios. He sits on the board of directors of the German beekeepers association (DBIB) and is vice president of the European Professional Beekeepers Association. And because griping is part of a lobbyist's trade, it is practically his professional duty to warn that "the very existence of beekeeping is at stake."

The problem, says Haefeker, has a number of causes, one being the varroa mite, introduced from Asia, and another is the widespread practice in agriculture of spraying wildflowers with herbicides and practicing monoculture. Another possible cause, according to Haefeker, is the controversial and growing use of genetic engineering in agriculture.

As far back as 2005, Haefeker ended an article he contributed to the journal *Der Kritischer Agrarbericht* (Critical Agricultural Report) with an Albert Einstein quote: "If the bee disappeared off the surface of the globe then man would only have four years of life left. No more bees, no more pollination, no more plants, no more animals, no more man."

Mysterious events in recent months [early 2007] have suddenly made Einstein's apocalyptic vision seem all the more topical. For unknown reasons, bee populations throughout Germany are disappearing—something that is so far only harming beekeepers. But the situation is different in the United States, where bees are dying in such dramatic numbers that the economic consequences could soon be dire. No one knows what is causing the bees to perish, but some experts believe that the large-scale use of genetically modified [GM] plants in the US could be a factor.

"If the bee disappeared off the surface of the globe then man would only have four years of life left."

Felix Kriechbaum, an official with a regional beekeepers association in Bavaria, recently reported a decline of almost 12 percent in local bee populations. When "bee populations disappear without a trace," says Kriechbaum, it is difficult to investigate the causes, because "most bees don't die in the beehive." There are many diseases that can cause bees to lose their sense of orientation so they can no longer find their way back to their hives.

Manfred Hederer, the president of the German beekeepers association, almost simultaneously reported a 25 percent drop in bee populations throughout Germany. In isolated cases, says Hederer, declines of up to 80 percent have been reported. He speculates that "a particular toxin, some agent with which we are not familiar," is killing the bees.

Ignored by Politicians

Politicians, until now, have shown little concern for such warnings or the woes of beekeepers. Although apiarists [that is, beekeepers] have been given a chance to make their case—for example in the run-up to the German cabinet's approval of a genetic engineering policy document by minister of agriculture Horst Seehofer in February—their complaints are still largely ignored.

Even when beekeepers actually go to court, as they recently did in a joint effort with the German chapter of the organic farming organization Demeter-International and other groups to oppose the use of genetically modified corn plants, they can only dream of the sort of media attention environmental organizations like Greenpeace attract with their protests at test sites.

[Between November 2006 and March 2007], the US has seen a decline in bee populations so dramatic that it eclipses all previous incidences of mass mortality.

But that could soon change. Since last November [2006], the US has seen a decline in bee populations so dramatic that it eclipses all previous incidences of mass mortality. Beekeepers on the East Coast of the United States complain that they have lost more than 70 percent of their stock since late last year, while the West Coast has seen a decline of up to 60 percent.

In an article in its business section in late February, the *New York Times* calculated the damage US agriculture would suffer if bees died out. Experts at Cornell University in upstate New York have estimated the value bees generate—by pollinating fruit and vegetable plants, almond trees and animal feed like clover—at more than $14 billion.

Scientists call the mysterious phenomenon "colony collapse disorder" (CCD), and it is fast turning into a national catastrophe of sorts. A number of universities and government agencies have formed a "CCD working group" to search for the causes of the calamity, but have so far come up empty-handed. But, like Dennis vanEngelsdorp, an apiarist with the Pennsylvania Department of Agriculture, they are already referring to the problem as a potential "AIDS for the bee industry."

The bacterial toxin in the genetically modified corn may have "altered the surface of the bees' intestines, sufficiently weakening the bees to allow the parasites to gain entry."

One thing is certain: Millions of bees have simply vanished. In most cases, all that's left in the hives are the doomed offspring. But dead bees are nowhere to be found—neither in nor anywhere close to the hives. Diana Cox-Foster, a member of the CCD working group, told the *Independent* that researchers were "extremely alarmed," adding that the crisis "has the potential to devastate the US beekeeping industry."

It is particularly worrisome, she said, that the bees' death is accompanied by a set of symptoms "which does not seem to match anything in the literature."

Colony Collapse Disorder

In many cases, scientists have found evidence of almost all known bee viruses in the few surviving bees found in the hives after most have disappeared. Some had five or six infections at the same time and were infested with fungi—a sign, experts say, that the insects' immune system may have collapsed.

The scientists are also surprised that bees and other insects usually leave the abandoned hives untouched. Nearby bee populations or parasites would normally raid the honey and

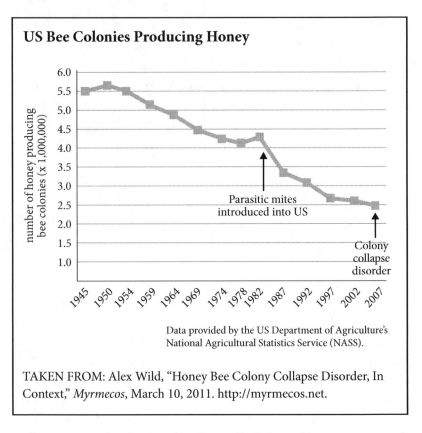

US Bee Colonies Producing Honey

Parasitic mites
introduced into US

Colony
collapse
disorder

Data provided by the US Department of Agriculture's
National Agricultural Statistics Service (NASS).

TAKEN FROM: Alex Wild, "Honey Bee Colony Collapse Disorder, In
Context," *Myrmecos*, March 10, 2011. http://myrmecos.net.

pollen stores of colonies that have died for other reasons, such
as excessive winter cold. "This suggests that there is something
toxic in the colony itself which is repelling them," says Cox-
Foster.

Walter Haefeker, the German beekeeping official, speculates that "besides a number of other factors," the fact that genetically modified, insect-resistant plants are now used in 40
percent of cornfields in the United States could be playing a
role. The figure is much lower in Germany—only 0.06 percent—and most of that occurs in the eastern states of
Mecklenburg-Western Pomerania and Brandenburg. Haefeker
recently sent a researcher at the CCD working group some
data from a bee study that he has long felt shows a possible
connection between genetic engineering and diseases in bees.

The study in question is a small research project conducted at the University of Jena from 2001 to 2004. The researchers examined the effects of pollen from a genetically modified maize variant called "Bt corn" on bees. A gene from a soil bacterium had been inserted into the corn that enabled the plant to produce an agent that is toxic to insect pests. The study concluded that there was no evidence of a "toxic effect of Bt corn on healthy honeybee populations." But when, by sheer chance, the bees used in the experiments were infested with a parasite, something eerie happened. According to the Jena study, a "significantly stronger decline in the number of bees" occurred among the insects that had been fed a highly concentrated Bt poison feed.

According to Hans-Hinrich Kaatz, a professor at the University of Halle[-Wittenberg] in eastern Germany and the director of the study, the bacterial toxin in the genetically modified corn may have "altered the surface of the bees' intestines, sufficiently weakening the bees to allow the parasites to gain entry—or perhaps it was the other way around. We don't know."

Of course, the concentration of the toxin was ten times higher in the experiments than in normal Bt corn pollen. In addition, the bee feed was administered over a relatively lengthy six-week period.

Kaatz would have preferred to continue studying the phenomenon but lacked the necessary funding. "Those who have the money are not interested in this sort of research," says the professor, "and those who are interested don't have the money."

There Is No Evidence That Bee Colony Crashes Worldwide Are Linked to Genetically Modified Crops

Jian J. Duan, Michelle Marvier, Joseph Huesing, Galen Dively, and Zachary Y. Huang

Jian J. Duan and Joseph Huesing are ecologists with Monsanto; Michelle Marvier is a professor at Santa Clara University; Galen Dively is a professor at the University of Maryland; and Zachary Y. Huang is a professor at Michigan State University. In the following viewpoint, the authors report on their meta-analysis, or study of previous studies, of the effect of genetically modified (GM) crops on the bee population. They conclude that there is no scientific evidence that GM crops harm bees.

As you read, consider the following questions:

1. Which groups of insects are targeted by the poisonous Cry proteins in GM crops, according to the authors?

2. How many studies do the authors say they have analyzed, and were these studies laboratory or field studies?

3. What stressors do the authors say might make bees more susceptible to the insecticides in GM crops?

Currently, all commercialized genetically engineered insect-resistant crops are based on crystalline (Cry) proteins encoded by genes derived from the soil-dwelling bacterium *Bacillus thuringiensis* (Bt). Studies on the mode of action and toxicology of Bt Cry proteins have established that these proteins are toxic to select groups of insects. Cry proteins currently produced in commercialized Bt crops target insects in the orders Lepidoptera (moths) and Coleoptera (beetles). Because of this specificity, most experts feel it is unlikely that these Bt crops would impact honeybee (Hymenoptera: *Apis mellifera* L.) populations. Nevertheless, because of their importance to agriculture—the economic value of honeybee pollination for U.S. agriculture has been estimated to be worth $0.15–19 billion per year—honeybees have been a key test species used in environmental safety assessments of Bt crops. These assessments have involved comparisons of honeybee larval and adult survival on purified Cry proteins or pollen collected from Bt crops versus survival on non-Bt control material.

Effects of Bt Crops on Honeybees

To date, no individual tests involving Bt crops or Cry proteins that target Lepidoptera or Coleoptera have shown significant impacts on honeybees. Despite this, there have been suggestions in the popular press that Bt proteins produced in insect-resistant crops might be contributing to recent declines in honeybee abundance. Given this speculation about potential adverse impacts of Bt crops on honeybees and the possibility that small sample sizes may have undermined the power of prior risk-assessment experiments, a formal meta-analysis, combining results from existing experiments, may provide more definitive answers. Meta-analysis increases statistical power and can reveal effects even when each of the individual studies failed to do so due to low replication. A recent meta-analysis, synthesizing results from 42 field studies involving Bt cotton and maize, did not examine effects on honeybees because very few studies have reported field data for this group. Here we report a meta-analysis of 25 laboratory studies [conducted on animals in a lab] that focused on the chronic and/or acute toxicity of Bt Cry proteins or Bt plant tissues (pollen) on honeybee larvae and adults. . . .

When all studies were combined, no statistically significant effect of Bt Cry protein treatments on survival of honeybees was detected. When data for lepidopteran-active and coleopteran-active Bt Cry proteins were compared using a fixed categorical meta-analysis model, the . . . pattern of no significant effects held true for each class of protein. No significant difference in effect sizes was detected between lepidopteran-active and coleopteran-active proteins. . . .

No significant effects on survival occurred with either larval or adult stages. This pattern was consistent when data from studies using lepidopteran-active and coleopteran-active Bt Cry proteins were analyzed either together or separately. No significant differences in effect sizes were detected between larvae and adults. . . .

> *The fact that laboratory studies typically expose honeybees to doses of Cry proteins that are ten or more times those encountered in the field provides additional reassurance that toxicity in the field is unlikely.*

No Effect on Bees

The lack of adverse effects of Bt Cry proteins on both larval and adult honeybees is consistent with prior studies on the activity spectrum and mode of action of different classes of Bt Cry proteins. To date, with the exception of a possible ant-specific Cry22 toxin patent application, no class of Bt Cry

Bees and Pollination

	Crop value in billions 2006	Percentage pollinated by honeybees	
Almonds	$2.2	100%	
Blueberries*	$0.5	90%	
Apples	$2.1	90%	
Peaches	$0.5	48%	
Oranges	$1.8	27%	
Cotton	$5.2	16%	
Soybeans	$19.7	5%	
Peanuts	$0.6	2%	
Strawberries	$1.5	2%	
Grapes	$3.2	1%	

*cultivated

These data come from the US Department of Agriculture and Roger A. Morse and Nicholas W. Calderone of Cornell University.

TAKEN FROM: *New York Times*, "Relying on Bees," February 27, 2007. www.nytimes.com.

protein has been found to be directly toxic to hymenopteran insects [that is, bees]. Although studies of acute toxicity performed in a laboratory setting may overlook sublethal or indirect effects that could potentially reduce the abundance of honeybees in a field setting, our findings strongly support the conclusion that the Cry proteins expressed in the current generation of Bt crops are unlikely to have adverse direct effects on the survival of honeybees. Additional analyses that included all available performance variables (survival, growth and development) similarly showed no adverse effect of Bt treatments. We do not report these results in depth here because they are potentially compromised by issues of noninde-pendence—it is inappropriate to simultaneously include mul-tiple measures taken on the same groups of bees. Unfortunately, few studies reported performance measures other than survival, and this prevented us from conducting separate analyses on these aspects of performance.

Although only laboratory data are synthesized here, the overall finding of no effect is consistent with the data available from a recent, well-replicated field study [conducted on ani-mals in the wild]. Additionally, the fact that laboratory studies typically expose honeybees to doses of Cry proteins that are ten or more times those encountered in the field provides ad-ditional reassurance that toxicity in the field is unlikely. How-ever, the need for additional studies in the field may be war-ranted if stressors [factors that cause stress to the bees] such as heat, pesticides, pathogens, and so on are suspected to alter the susceptibility of honeybees to Cry protein toxicity.

Genetically Modified Mosquitoes May Help Eradicate Dengue Fever in Malaysia

Sarah Cumberland

Sarah Cumberland is the editor of the Bulletin of the World Health Organization. *In the following viewpoint, she reports that dengue fever is a dangerous illness spread by mosquitoes. She says scientists hope to genetically manipulate male mosquitoes so that their offspring die, reducing mosquito populations and thus reducing the spread of dengue fever. Cumberland says that tests are moving forward in Malaysia, where dengue fever is a serious health problem. Cumberland also emphasizes the importance of working with individual nations to assure people that releasing the genetically modified (GM) mosquitoes is safe.*

As you read, consider the following questions:

1. According to Cumberland, how many people are affected by dengue fever each year and what vaccines and cures are available?

2. What does Cumberland say is the next stage of GM mosquito testing in Malaysia?

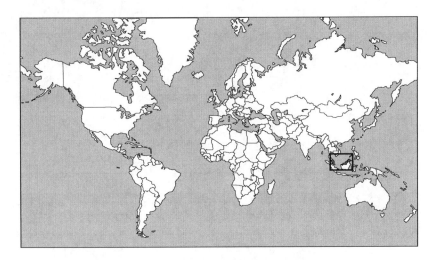

3. What are the process and effects of population replacement techniques in controlling insect populations through genetic modification, according to Cumberland?

Dengue fever is a disease that afflicts an estimated 100 million people per year. There is no vaccine and no cure. The mosquito-borne viral infection causes severe flu-like illness, often requiring hospitalization, and can develop into the potentially fatal dengue haemorrhagic fever.

Fight the Mosquito

Experts agree that the only successful way to control or prevent this disease is to combat its vector [that is, the way in which it is spread, by mosquitoes]. But this task is extremely difficult as the *Aedes* mosquito genus thrives in urban settings and bites during the day. Its eggs can lie dormant in dried-up water receptacles, such as in car tyres, which are often shipped around the world.

Fortunately a new front is forming in the battle against this tenacious mosquito as years of scientific work come to fruition. In the next year [2009] or two, if biosafety, regulatory and ethical approvals and community consent are obtained, a new kind of mosquito could be released into the environment.

Created in the laboratories of Oxford University and Oxitec [Oxford Insect Technologies], a biotechnology company located in the south of England, these male mosquitoes of the *Aedes aegypti* species will be on a mission to mate, but not to breed.

They are in fact designed to cause the wild females with whom they mate to produce offspring that die at the pupa stage with the aim of significantly reducing the native population below the numbers required to sustain dengue fever transmission.

Insect population suppression—employing what is known as sterile insect technique—has actually been used to control agricultural pests for more than 50 years by releasing laboratory-reared insects made sterile through irradiation. Native females that mate with the sterile males produce nonviable offspring, leading to a decline in the natural population. The governments of Guatemala, Mexico and the United States of America (USA) irradiate some two billion male Mediterranean fruit flies every week, before releasing them into the wild to mate. Another agricultural pest, the parasitic screwworm, has in this way been eradicated from the USA and much of Central America.

But this technique has not been successfully used against mosquitoes because sterilizing doses of radiation weaken them, reducing their ability to compete for mates, which is fundamental to the method—until now. Luke Alphey, founder and research director of Oxitec, working with colleagues at Oxford University, discovered that by inserting a single gene into the *A. aegypti*'s DNA, it was possible to produce males whose offspring do not survive to adulthood.

Oxitec's findings have now been successfully corroborated through the world's first semi-field trials held in collaboration with the Institute for Medical Research (IMR) in Malaysia. These trials were held in a confined field house that mimicked the natural environment and aimed to test the GM [genetically modified] male's mating competitiveness with unmodified insects.

Insect population suppression . . . has actually been used to control agricultural pests for more than 50 years.

Malaysia Is in the Lead

Malaysia, which has almost 50,000 reported cases of dengue fever per year, has also taken a lead in risk assessment of GM mosquitoes. The Academy of Sciences in Malaysia has conducted an independent review of these semi-field trials and has recommended that the project proceed to the next step once it has passed regulatory and ethical clearances. In December 2008, international experts took part in a meeting convened by the United Nations Development Programme (UNDP) at IMR to discuss risk assessment with Malaysian and regional scientists and regulators.

The next stage will be to conduct open-release trials in which the mosquitoes are released into selected, naturally contained sites such as islands. According to Dr Yeya Touré, manager of innovative vector control interventions at the UNDP/World Bank/World Health Organization (WHO) Special Programme for Research and Training in Tropical Diseases (TDR), these trials may be just "a matter of months away".

"We are no longer talking about wild speculation," says Alphey. "If the funds are made available, I can see the elimination of dengue from regions or groups of countries using GM technology integrated with other tools." Good news for the 2.5 billion people currently at risk of the disease.

Since 1970, there has been a surge in dengue fever epidemics with more than 100 countries worldwide now seriously affected. Increased shipping of goods and urbanization have been blamed for the introduction and spread of the *Aedes* mosquito into the Americas and southeastern Asia.

According to a study conducted by the Indian Institute of Management in Ahmedabad, *Aedes* mosquito-borne disease—primarily dengue fever and Chikungunya, another viral disease—costs India alone a hefty US$1.3 billion every year, 95% of that due to illness.

> *"If the funds are made available, I can see the elimination of dengue from regions or groups of countries using GM technology integrated with other tools."*

But it's not only the *Aedes* mosquito and dengue control that are under the microscope. According to Paul Eggleston at Keele University in England, who has been working on developing GM mosquitoes since 1983, it is now possible to genetically modify all major taxonomic groups of mosquito, including those of the *Anopheles* genus, which is the vector of malaria, and those of the *Culex* genus, the vector of lymphatic filariasis, which can lead to elephantiasis. The potential for a concerted push-back against mosquito-borne diseases is enormous.

Suppression vs. Replacement

It is important to make the distinction between population suppression using a sterile insect technique—Oxitec's approach—and another approach, known as population replacement, which is under development. This more technically challenging strategy modifies the insect so that it can no longer transmit the parasite that causes dengue. It relies on GM insects mating with and permanently altering the genetic makeup of the wild population.

While prototypes of some of the necessary components have performed well in laboratory settings, population re-

---

Mosquitoes and Dengue Transmission

The mosquitoes acquire the [dengue] virus when they feed on a viremic human (someone who is already infected with dengue virus). The mosquito is capable of transmitting dengue if it immediately bites another host or after eight to 12 days of viral replication in its salivary glands, known as an extrinsic incubation period. The mosquito remains infected for the remainder of its 15- to 65-day life span. Vertical transmission of dengue virus in mosquitoes has been documented, which means that infected mosquitoes can pass the virus on to their young. The eggs of *Aedes* mosquitoes are able to withstand long periods of desiccation (dryness), reportedly as long as one year.

Tirtha Chakraborty,
Dengue Fever and Other Hemorrhagic Viruses.
New York: Chelsea House, 2008.

---

placement is several years away from field trial. "There are no plans to release insects into the wild yet," says Eggleston. "As scientists, we are aware of the need to take a cautious approach. We want to be as sure as we can possibly be that the health benefit is unambiguous."

TDR's Touré concurs: "These [GM] mosquitoes have to replace the wild population," he says. "We have to be sure that they are not going to introduce any other issues through their genetic modification."

Oxitec's Alphey is hopeful that his non-propagating, non-biting (because they are males) GM mosquitoes will be given the "thumbs-up", but he is well aware of the importance of winning over the sceptics if GM-based sterilization is to become a significant public health tool. "We have to provide the necessary information to allow the scientists and technical advisers to governments in affected countries to decide whether this is right for their country and circumstances," he says.

Those local scientists should also be involved in the development of the technology so that they can help their governments to make informed decisions and weigh up the potential benefits and risks. Scientists will also be needed to implement the strategies, to work in laboratories that will rear and distribute the GM mosquitoes in their local settings.

In recognition of WHO's role in providing guidance, a technical consultation will be held in May [2009] in Geneva [Switzerland] to assess the current status and discuss future plans for developing GM mosquitoes as a control tool. Co-organized with the Foundation for the National Institutes of Health, the consultation will bring together experts in global biotechnology, safety and GM research, as well as regulatory and policy officials from WHO member states. "The meeting will cover issues such as biosafety assessment, regulatory, ethics and the social aspects of research," explains Touré. The technical consultation will be followed by a broader public consultation that will be attended by nongovernmental organizations and advocacy groups, as well as media representatives.

Local scientists should also be involved in the development of the technology so that they can help their governments to make informed decisions and weigh up the potential benefits and risks.

Despite all the buzz about GM mosquitoes, few believe they represent a silver bullet against mosquito-borne diseases. Alphey himself sees GM as part of an overall disease management system, a view echoed by Anthony James, who is working on population replacement at the University of California: "If any one of these GM techniques works, we don't expect it will provide the solution alone," he says. "We are going to have to develop a very strong integration of the components of [mosquito-borne disease] eradication: vector control, vaccines and drugs," he says.

And as Eggleston points out: "The problem isn't going to go away. Global warming is having a real impact, with the encroachment of mosquito-borne diseases on new territory, including southern Europe."

The Release of Genetically Modified Mosquitoes in Malaysia Is Dangerous and Must Be Stopped

Consumers Association of Penang

The Consumers Association of Penang (CAP) is a consumer advocacy organization in Malaysia that focuses on ecological and social justice issues. In the following viewpoint, CAP reports that genetically modified (GM) mosquitoes are to be released into the wild in Malaysia in the hope that the mosquitoes will reduce dengue fever. CAP argues that the effects of releasing GM mosquitoes into the wild in Malaysia are unknown and potentially dangerous. CAP says the proposed tests have not been subject to sufficient oversight, and the organization concludes that the tests should be aborted.

As you read, consider the following questions:

1. Why were the initial field tests of GM mosquitoes delayed, according to CAP?
2. Why does GeneWatch UK believe that the novelty of the application of GM technology has hurt the regulatory process?

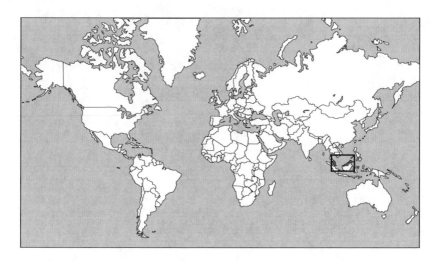

3. Why does CAP say that the release of the mosquitoes in Malaysia must be seen as a worldwide release?

CAP [Consumers Association of Penang] and Sahabat Alam Malaysia (SAM) [Friends of the Earth, Malaysia] call upon the National Biosafety Board (NBB) to revoke the approval given to the Institute for Medical Research (IMR) in October 2010 to release genetically modified (GM) male *Aedes aegypti* mosquitoes for the purpose of a field experiment.

A Dangerous Test

The applicant and implementer of the field trial is the IMR which had developed the GM mosquitoes in a joint research with [United Kingdom] UK-based biotech company Oxitec [Oxford Insect Technologies]. The field trial which was supposed to be carried out last December [2010] in uninhabited and inhabited sites in the districts of Bentong, Pahang and Alor Gajah, Melaka, was reportedly delayed because of bad weather.

Following the NBB's decision, CAP and SAM had submitted a memorandum to the Malaysian government on 20 December 2010 raising our concerns on serious ethical, legal, public health and human rights issues. Twenty-nine organizations in Malaysia and 87 civil society organizations throughout the world, concerned by the impending release of the GM mosquitoes, had also raised their apprehension in open letters to the authorities.

Malaysia will be the first country to release this particular strain of GM *Aedes aegypti* mosquitoes OX513A (My1). The only other country which has released GM *Aedes* mosquitoes with the same transgenic construct is the Cayman Islands—a British overseas territory. In November 2010, international reports had revealed that Oxitec publicly announced its GM *Aedes* mosquitoes' field trials in the Cayman Islands only one year after the event.

The field releases in the Cayman Islands in 2009 and 2010 were controversial and calls have been made for a transparent assessment of the full, long-term health and environmental impacts of these trials in the Cayman Islands, pending which, no further field releases of GM mosquitoes should occur anywhere else.

Besides this, GeneWatch UK, a science-based not-for-profit organisation, has conducted and published an investigation of Oxitec's role in the development, patenting and promotion of the use of these genetically modified (GM) mosquitoes.

The fact that this project involves the creation and propagation of a deadly insect and its eventual release in the natural environment means that it is a dangerous and risky enterprise.

GeneWatch UK is concerned that the novelty of this application of GM technology has made regulators in several countries too dependent on advice provided by Oxitec which has a vested interest in speeding its products into the marketplace in order to generate financial returns for its investors. In Gene-

Watch UK's view this means that a number of potential risks have been omitted or downplayed. . . .

The fact that this project involves the creation and propagation of a deadly insect and its eventual release in the natural environment means that it is a dangerous and risky enterprise.

A Worldwide Danger

The GM mosquitoes will be released into a complicated ecosystem, involving other mosquito species, predators and prey, the dengue virus, and the humans who are bitten. Because this system is poorly understood, there remain unanswered questions about the impacts of the proposed releases.

The outcome of this experiment is thus unpredictable and largely unknown. If the unintended occurs in the environment, these releases would be impossible to monitor, contain or mitigate, and they are irreversible.

Mosquitoes, natural or engineered, do not respect national borders. It is not possible for any country to control mosquitoes from crossing their borders in this age of air travel and large-scale movements of people and materials. For this reason, releasing a GM mosquito must be considered as a worldwide release as it will potentially affect every nation on the planet. Hence, were Malaysia's neighbouring countries such as Singapore, Indonesia and Thailand officially informed about the impending release?

Given the unpredictable consequences and potential risks, the chances of things going wrong cannot be overstated. Why are we allowing ourselves to be guinea pigs for this doubtful technology? What if the experiment does not go according to plan and something goes terribly wrong with the release? First and foremost, Oxitec will not be wholly liable as IMR is the applicant for the release.

It is regrettable that the authorities seem intent on allowing the trials to go ahead, despite public calls to be cautious and to take into account the precautionary approach [referring to the principle that says the burden of proof to show an action is *not* harmful falls on those undertaking the action] based on valid concerns. That we are dealing with GM insects, especially disease-carrying mosquitoes on which there are very few guidelines for biosafety assessment simply because there is very little information to go on, should be a push for the precautionary approach.

Why are we allowing ourselves to be guinea pigs for this doubtful technology?

Malaysia should uphold transparency, rigorous scientific standards, the precautionary principle, justice and human rights, and ethical and lawful practices. Otherwise, we will be opening the floodgates for foreign corporations to dump in Malaysia other GM insects, crops, food, feed and processing in the future. What is at stake is the health of Malaysians and our neighbours, our environment and biological diversity.

We hereby call upon the NBB in consultation with the Genetic Modification Advisory Committee to review and revoke the approval for the field release of these GM mosquitoes as allowed for under the Biosafety Act 2007.

The United States Faces Credible Threats from Genetically Modified Germ Warfare

Jerry Warner, James Ramsbotham, Ewelina Tunia, and James J. Valdes

Jerry Warner is managing director of Defense Life Sciences, LLC; James Ramsbotham is president of Orion Enterprises, Inc.; and Ewelina Tunia is a research assistant and James J. Valdes is a senior research fellow, both at the National Defense University's Center for Technology and National Security Policy. In the following viewpoint, the authors argue that creating genetically modified (GM) bioweapons is difficult and would require the resources of a nation-state. Nonetheless, the authors conclude that there is a real threat that GM bioweapons could be created and used against the United States.

As you read, consider the following questions:

1. What are three arguments for the likelihood of a catastrophic biological attack listed by the authors?

2. According to the authors, what is the likelihood of developing a completely artificial biological weapon versus the likelihood of modifying an existent pathogen?

Jerry Warner, James Ramsbotham, Ewelina Tunia, and James J. Valdes, "Analysis of the Threat of Genetically Modified Organisms for Biological Warfare," Center for Technology and National Security Policy, National Defense University, May 2011, pp. 3, 5–7, 21, 29–30. Reproduced by permission.

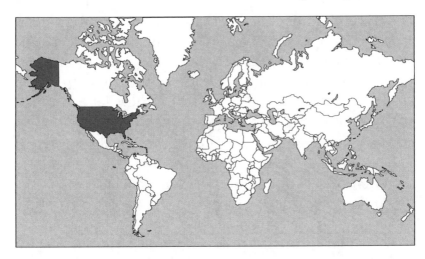

3. Why do the authors believe that identifying and preventing any GMO attack will be problematic?

Evaluating the potential threats posed by advances in biotechnology, especially genetically modified organisms (GMOs) and synthetic biology remains a contentious issue. Some believe that, inevitably, these advances will lead to a catastrophic biological attack. Others believe that, despite these advances, the scientific and technical requirements, as well as the fundamental laws of natural selection will prevent such an attack.

Catastrophic Biological Attack

To better understand this issue, this study narrowed the scope of consideration in several dimensions. First, our analysis primarily focused on what we defined as a "catastrophic biological attack," with a required level of damage more associated with biological warfare than bioterrorism. [We define a catastrophic biowarfare attack as one having *direct* physical scale, such as the loss of a major U.S. city or national system.] This damage would need to be *direct* in nature where the effect is more physical than psychological. Second, this biological attack would be restricted to the United States, not another nation or entity. In this sense, U.S. geography, climatology, infrastructure and medical systems play to counterbalance any potential biological attack. Even within a more narrow scope, there remains inherent complexity and uncertainty which, combined with the considerable rate of change for biotechnology, defies a simple, straightforward answer.

We approached the issue by establishing an "Analytical Framework"—a baseline of the technical requirements to "play" in the field of GMOs at the scale of biological warfare. The primary focus of the framework are those aspects of the technology directly affecting humans by inducing virulent infectious disease, or through expression of toxins or suppression of the immune response of target subjects. Parallel threats exist for animals and plants in the food chain and, secondarily, in the ecosphere. Although not specifically included in this analysis, those threats can also be evaluated within the analytical framework. To establish our analytical framework, we focused on the engineering of novel single-cell microorganisms previously unknown in nature as described by four conditions:

1. Modification of known pathogen [that is, harmful] microorganisms to new functionalities

2. Modification of nonpathogens to become pathogenic

3. Synthesizing pathogenic microorganisms *de novo* [that is, from scratch]

4. Synthesizing completely artificial or "abiotic" pathogenic "cells" or biomolecules.

We conclude that, broadly stated, peaceful scientific advances, global statistics and demographics of GMOs suggest that the potential for corruption of biotechnology to catastrophic malevolent use is considerable. At a more detailed level, we find that there are tangible opportunities for many potential adversaries to acquire, modify and then manufacture to scale a potential GMO pathogen. Further development of a modified pathogen for use in a full-scale direct catastrophic biological attack is feasible, but the full spectrum of technologies for scale-up, testing, packaging, weapon production and employment will most likely require the resources of a nation-state or comparably resourced organization. . . .

The potential for corruption of biotechnology to catastrophic malevolent use is considerable.

What Is the Issue?

Evaluating the potential threat posed by advances in biotechnology, especially genetically modified organisms (GMOs), and synthetic biology remains a contentious issue. The rapid development of the tools of molecular biology and metabolic engineering has enabled the development of chimeric organisms [that is, composed of genetic material from multiple creatures] which possess characteristics which are not native to the wild variant. This is commonplace in the area of bio-manufacturing, where genes are introduced into organisms such as *E. coli* and products manufactured via large-scale fermentation. More recently, entire metabolic pathways, albeit of limited complexity, have been engineered into organisms, for example, for the production of artemisinin [an antimalarial drug] in yeast. In addition to such metabolic engineering projects, whole genomes are being sequenced, leading to the possibility of creating organisms *de novo*.

Numerous lectures, briefings and articles have argued that the dual-use nature of biotechnology [for peaceful and military purposes], the training of foreign students in American universities and the easy availability of information on the Internet have given potential adversaries access to biological weapons of unimagined [deadliness] which pose an existential threat. Some believe that, inevitably, these advances will lead to a catastrophic biological attack.

Others have argued the opposite that making all information publicly available will enable a more universal "white biotechnology" which will ultimately monitor the field and provide the means to defeat any threat developed by adversaries. It has been argued that, despite these advances, the scientific and technical requirements, as well as the fundamental laws of natural selection, will prevent such an attack.

[Many] have argued that the dual-use nature of biotechnology, the training of foreign students in American universities and the easy availability of information on the Internet have given potential adversaries access to biological weapons.

An example of the controversy is represented by statements such as that found on the website of the Hastings Center, which states that, "Research suggests that synthetic biology may soon be a technology of choice for a nation or terrorist hoping to develop or acquire a pathogen for use as a weapon," however, without explicit supporting references.

To further demonstrate the depth of the issue, a brief listing of the current arguments for/against the likelihood of a catastrophic biological attack being brought about by advances in synthetic biology follows.

Arguments *for* include:

- Advances in the science and technology of genetics, writ large.
- Growth of commercial GMO activities.
- GMO knowledge base and its availability.
- Simplicity and availability of required low-cost materials and equipment.

- Human abuse of antibiotics and other practices which make populations more vulnerable to a GMO.

- Occurrences of pandemic disease derived from natural genetic evolution.

Arguments *against* include:

- Given the complexity of living organisms and their genetic makeup and responses, it is extremely difficult to predict the outcome of any genetic modification.

- The very limited success of "gene therapy"—peaceful medical objectives of genetics for new therapeutics and "individualized" gene-based treatments are as yet unrealized.

- Nature is intolerant of modifications or new organisms and tends to select against them. Natural evolutionary processes make/break GMOs continually for the last three billion years, and it is unlikely that humans will outdo that.

- Extreme technical difficulties of "weaponization" for most potential GMO pathogens.

- An unimpressive history of bioterrorist attacks. . . .

Key Questions

1. What is the nature and scope of the threat, if any, posed by GMOs, to include the potential to develop completely *de novo* organisms or completely artificial abiotic systems?

2. What are the fundamental processes and global state of the art for creating GMOs?

3. Beyond the technical means to create a GMO, what might the follow-on requirements for "weaponization" include?

The Cost of Equipping a Genetic Engineering Lab That Could Produce Bioweapons

The cost of a biolab is expensive, but not prohibitive compared to, for example, a nuclear plant.

Capability	Basic	Enhanced
Gene Sequencer (Refurbished 48 Capillary ABi 373)		$25,000
Gene Synthesizer (Polyplex 96-well plate high speed synthesizer)	$4,000	$65,000
ABi 392 DNA/RNA synthesizer/96 Well High Speed		$1,500
PCR Synthesizer		
Fermentor/bioreactor	$5,000	
Automated controller for Bioreactor		$8,500
High Quality Glove Boxes (2)	$4,000	$6,000
CO_2 Incubator (Basic for Viruses)	$6,000	$19,000
Cell factory or roller bottles, Basic for Viruses	$3,000	$24,000
Dryer/lyophilizer (Laboratory size <15 L capacity)	$15,000	$45,000
Refrigerator/Freezer (Large)	$3,000	$15,000
General laboratory equipment, pH meter, centrifuge, balance, temperature controlled water baths, etc.	$10,000	$10,000
Reagents, restriction enzymes, expendable supplies, etc.	$10,000	$15,000
Total	$60,000	$234,000

TAKEN FROM: Jerry Warner et al., *Analysis of the Threat of Genetically Modified Organisms for Biological Warfare*, Center for Technology and National Security Policy, National Defense University, May 2011.

4. What are the capabilities and incentives for foreign states, transnational groups, small terrorist groups, or individuals to attempt to develop a significant GMO threat?. . .

Using the original set of research questions posed, we found:

1. Primary question: What is the nature and scope of the threat, if any, posed by GMOs, to include the potential to develop completely *de novo* organisms or completely artificial abiotic systems?

- The likelihood of a completely artificial or abiotic single-cell entity, much less a deliberate pathogen, is very small. To date, despite some published claims of an artificial life-form, biological science is, at most, still only emulating the otherwise natural fabrication of living entities.

- Modification of existing pathogens to avoid detection, be more virulent or better weaponized is more likely, but probably only in the hands of a nation-state or above level. Overall, the overhead to create/use GMOs as a military weapon is only plausible at nation-state or above level.

2. What are the fundamental processes and global state of the art for creating GMOs?. . . Due to the significant global increases in the field of biotechnology, the primary capabilities to at least create one GMO culture is widely available.

3. Beyond the technical means to create a GMO, what might the follow-on requirements for "weaponization" include?

- Outside the laboratory, nature tends to side with the defender since ambient conditions tend to kill or reduce effectiveness of GMOs. Evolutionary processes suppress man-made efforts to propagate pandemic-like weapons. Nonetheless, as in nature, exceptions occur. Sunlight (UV), heat, cold, lack of availability of a suitable host organism, all comes into play; therefore,

- The ability of most perpetrators to manufacture scale quantities (nominally 25 gallons) is apparent. However the final steps of pathogen stabilization and delivery will elude all but the very competent nation-state adversary.

4. What are the capabilities and incentives for foreign states, transnational groups, small terrorist groups, or individuals to attempt to develop a significant GMO threat?

Although possession of a capability to develop a GMO threat is plausible by a non-nation actor, other than using GMO to avoid detection, there is no real advantage to do so and mounting a "catastrophic" pathogen attack is more easily accomplished without GMO overhead and uncertainties. . . .

Identifying and preventing any GMO attack will be problematic.

Other relevant findings include:

- There is a trade space for some pathogens where increased virulence will result in "burn-out" within a confined geographical area, that is, those susceptible to the pathogen will succumb quickly, while those who aren't will be immune. The propagation of the pathogen will then cease unless individuals break out of the confined area and further communicate the disease to new areas.

- Identifying and preventing any GMO attack will be problematic. Unlike other classes of weapons (e.g., nuclear devices, artillery pieces, etc.) the science, technology, means of production and delivery of GMOs are demonstrably dual use. The path necessary to produce a beneficial GMO for commerce is often indistinguishable from that necessary to create something malevolent, and the path from a beneficial to a threat GMO is short and swift. The GMO threat generally cannot be detected by the normal intelligence collection and analysis methods.

Periodical and Internet Sources Bibliography

The following articles have been selected to supplement the diverse views presented in this chapter.

Busani Bafana — "Modified Banana Could Cure Deadly Disease," *Inter Press Service*, August 12, 2010. http://ipsnews.net.

Mark Q. Benedict and Helen Wallace — "Should Scientists Use Genetically Modified Insects to Fight Disease?," *Scientific American*, October 24, 2011.

Malcolm Dando — "Science, Technology, and the Bioweapons Treaty," *Bulletin of the Atomic Scientist*, May 13, 2011.

Patty Donovan — "Genetically Modified Crops Implicated in Honeybee Colony Collapse Disorder," Natural News Network, January 11, 2009. www.naturalnews.com.

Frank Jordans — "Clinton Warns of Bioweapon Threat from Gene Tech," MSNBC, December 7, 2011. www.msnbc.msn.com.

Alexis Madrigal — "Bee Colony Collapse May Have Several Causes," *Wired*, January 8, 2010.

Rosli Omar — "GM Mosquito Trial: A Dangerous Precedent," Malaysiakini, September 13, 2010. www.malaysiakini.com.

Andrew Pollack — "GM Mosquito Fights Dengue by Killing Its Own," *Times of India*, November 1, 2011.

Ian Sample — "Genetically Modified Mosquitoes Lined Up to Tackle Dengue Fever," *Guardian*, November 11, 2010.

David Tribe — "Bt Corn Cleared in Honey Bee Colony Collapse Disorder," *GMO Pundit* (blog), May 1, 2007. http://gmopundit.blogspot.com.

Genetic Engineering and Animals

Genetically Modified Salmon Show Promise as a Food Source in the United States

The Economist

The Economist *is a British business and world affairs publication. In the following viewpoint, the* Economist *reports that researchers in the United States are developing a version of a trout with large amounts of muscle and another of a salmon that grows to large size quickly. The hope, the* Economist *says, is that such fish will be a lucrative meat source that will benefit both consumers and fish farmers. Some critics are worried that genetically modified (GM) salmon may escape into the wild and drive non-GM salmon to extinction, but the* Economist *says that scientists have sterilized GM salmon to prevent this from occurring.*

As you read, consider the following questions:

1. Acccording to the *Economist*, what is the Belgian Blue?
2. What regulator does the *Economist* say must sign off on AquaBounty's fish, and how long has AquaBounty been petitioning them?
3. What have humans done to the environment that might make it possible for GM salmon to put pressure on natural salmon in the wild, according to the viewpoint?

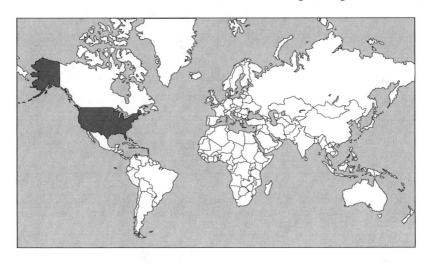

The Belgian Blue is an ugly but tasty cow that has 40% more muscle than it should have. It is the product of random mutation followed by selective breeding—as, indeed, are all domesticated creatures. But where an old art has led, a new one may follow. By understanding which genetic changes have been consolidated in the Belgian Blue, it may be possible to design and build similar versions of other species using genetic engineering as a shortcut. That is precisely what Terry Bradley, a fish biologist at the University of Rhode Island, is trying to do. Instead of cattle, he is doing it in trout. His is one of two projects that may soon put the first biotech animals on the dinner table.

More Muscle

Belgian Blues are so big because their genes for a protein called myostatin, a hormone that regulates muscle growth, do not work properly. Dr Bradley has launched a four-pronged attack on the myostatin in his trout. First, he has introduced a gene that turns out a stunted version of the myostatin receptor, the molecule that sits in the surface membrane of muscle cells and receives the message to stop growing. The stunted receptor does not pass the message on properly. He has also added two genes for nonfunctional variants of myostatin. These churn out proteins which bind to the receptors, swamping and diluting the effect of functional myostatin molecules. Finally, he has added a gene that causes overproduction of another protein, follistatin. This binds to myostatin and renders it inoperative.

The upshot of all this tinkering is a trout that has twice the abdominal muscle mass of its traditional counterparts. Moreover, this muscle is low in fat, like that of its bovine counterparts. That, and the fact that the animal's other organs are unaffected, means it does not take twice as much food to grow a fish to maturity.

The genetic engineers at AquaBounty [Technologies], a company based in Waltham, Massachusetts, have taken a different route using a different species. They are trying to grow supersize salmon by tinkering with the genes for growth hormone. Two snippets of DNA are involved. One, taken from a relative of the cod called the ocean pout, promotes the activity of the gene that encodes growth hormone. The other, taken from a Chinook salmon, is a version of the growth-hormone gene itself. Unmodified salmon undergo a period of restricted growth when they are young. Together these two pieces of DNA produce growth hormone during that lull, abolishing it. The result is a fish that reaches marketable size in 18–24 months, as opposed to 30 months for the normal variety.

The upshot of all this tinkering is a trout that has twice the abdominal muscle mass of its traditional counterparts.

It is one thing to make such fish, of course. It is quite another to get them to market. First, it is necessary to receive the approval of the regulators. In America the regulator in question is the Food and Drug Administration [FDA], which AquaBounty says it has been petitioning for more than a de-

"Don't tell me she's not transgenic," cartoon by Steve Harris, www.CartoonStock.com. Copyright © Steve Harris. Reproduction rights obtainable from www.CartoonStock.com.

cade and which published guidelines for approving genetically engineered animals in 2009. AquaBounty has now filed its remaining studies for approval, and hopes to hear the result this year [2010]. Dr Bradley has not yet applied for approval.

Competing in the Wild

It seems unlikely that either of the new procedures will yield something that is unsafe to eat. But what happens if the creatures escape and start breeding in the wild? For that to be a problem, the modified fish would have to be better at surviving and reproducing than those honed by millions of years of natural selection. On the face of it, this seems unlikely, because the characteristics that have been engineered into them are ones designed to make them into better food, rather than lean, mean breeding machines.

But there is a chink [weak spot] in this argument. As Mark Abrahams, a biologist at Memorial University in Newfoundland, points out, it is not just the fish that have been modified by man, but also the environment in which they could escape. Many of the creatures that eat salmon and trout, such as bears and some birds, have had their ranks thinned by human activity. Dr Abrahams thinks it possible that fast-growing salmon could displace the natural sort in places where predators are rare.

It seems unlikely that either of the new procedures will yield something that is unsafe to eat.

AquaBounty is addressing such concerns by subjecting developing eggs to high pressures. This alters their complement of chromosomes, giving them three sets per cell instead of the usual two. Such "triploid" fish are perfectly viable, but they are sterile. Only a small, sequestered breeding stock is allowed to remain diploid. The company claims a 99% success rate with its pressurising technique which, according to John Buchanan, its research director, meets the FDA's requirements. As for the trout, Dr Bradley says his fish have enough trouble breeding on their own for it to be unlikely that they would do well in the wild. To get them to lay eggs and produce milt (seminal fluid) you have to squeeze them by hand. But he says his fish could also be made triploid if necessary.

Whether people will actually want to buy or eat the new fish is another question—though they buy the meat of Belgian Blue cattle at a premium. If people will pay extra for meat from a monstrosity like the Belgian Blue, anything is possible.

Canada Should Regulate Dangerous Genetically Modified Salmon

Alex Atamanenko

Alex Atamanenko is a Canadian politician in the New Democratic Party and a member of Parliament for British Columbia Southern Interior. In the following viewpoint, he argues that genetically modified (GM) salmon, if released in the wild, could pose a threat to natural salmon and thus to Canadian ecology and economy. Atamanenko argues that the Canadian government has been secretive about the safety of the GM salmon. He concludes that the government must be more transparent and that a moratorium should be declared on the development of GM animals.

As you read, consider the following questions:

1. According to Atamanenko, what is the business plan of AquaBounty Technologies?
2. Which US agency does not believe the GM salmon are safe, and what dangers does it identify, according to Atamanenko?
3. What does Atamanenko believe is the gorilla in the room when it comes to containing GM technologies?

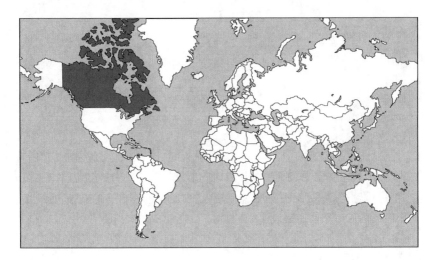

AquaBounty Technologies (AT), headquartered in the US, has genetically modified (GM) a faster growing Atlantic salmon by inserting a growth hormone gene from Chinook salmon and genetic material from the eel-like ocean pout. The company's business plan is to produce genetically modified salmon eggs in Prince Edward Island (PEI), ship the eggs for grow out and processing in Panama and then sell a "table ready" product into the US consumer market.

Government Secrecy

AquaBounty says that the fish will be sterile but can only guarantee that 95% of the salmon will be unable to reproduce. Even worse, the company's own data reveals this fish has less omega-3 and omega-6 fatty acids than regular farmed salmon and doesn't taste as good.

Due to a technicality, the US House of Representatives recently voted to block the US Food and Drug Administration (FDA) approval of genetically modified salmon. The Conservative [Canadian] government, with its usual air of secrecy, is still refusing to disclose whether the company has asked for approvals in Canada.

The FDA is regulating GE [genetically engineered] animals as "new animal drugs", however, the approval process lacks transparency. The FDA's preliminary conclusion was that the GM salmon is safe to eat and poses no environmental risk, however, the [Canadian] Department of Fisheries and Oceans (DFO) has contradicted this assessment and acknowledged that GM salmon could pose a significant risk to wild fish stocks.

According to Dr. Michael Hansen, senior scientist at Consumers Union, AT used insensitive tests to try and measure the GM salmon's levels of growth hormone and the levels of IGF-1, a hormone linked to a number of cancers. "The FDA is relying on woefully inadequate data. There is sloppy science, small sample sizes, and questionable practices."

According to a report by the National Academy of Sciences, the inability to identify all potential problems early on and the difficulty of trying to solve problems after they arise are the greatest science-based concerns when it comes to the environmental issues surrounding GM animals. In the face of such uncertainty, how can posing such a threat to thousands of years of Mother Nature's work be in any way justified?

"The FDA is relying on woefully inadequate data. There is sloppy science, small sample sizes, and questionable practices."

A Danger in the Wild

Wild salmon is carnivorous and the fast-growing GM salmon could consume up to five times more food than other farmed salmon. Any risk of them escaping into the wild is completely unacceptable. Mature farmed Atlantic salmon have already escaped their nets and been recorded in streams in BC [British Columbia]. Human negligence and error is always the gorilla in the room when it comes to containing GM technologies.

NDP [New Democratic Party] Fin Donnelly, MP [member of Parliament] will be reintroducing his motion which asks the government to explain its regulations and to set up a system to notify Canadians about any requests for approvals and approval decisions. The motion also asks the government to "prevent the introduction of genetically modified salmon destined for human consumption into the Canadian food system until further scientific studies are concluded by the relevant departments to determine the impact of genetically modified salmon on human health and on the health of marine species, ecosystems and habitats."

Canadians have not been asked for their views on GM animals, and it is clear that our regulations are not keeping up with the pace of GM technologies.

The aquaculture industry does not support the commercialization of GM fish because there is no market demand. In 2010 over 60 fisheries and oceans conservation, environmental and social justice groups signed a joint statement opposing GM fish.

Canadians have not been asked for their views on GM animals, and it is clear that our regulations are not keeping up with the pace of GM technologies. I hope you will join me in calling for a moratorium on genetically engineered higher life-forms pending the outcome of a nationwide consultation about the ethical implications of embarking down this inherently risky road.

Cloning May Allow the Preservation of Endangered Animals

Raul E. Piña-Aguilar, Janet Lopez-Saucedo, Richard Sheffield, Lilia I. Ruiz-Galaz, Jose de J. Barroso-Padilla, and Antonio Gutiérrez-Gutiérrez

Raul E. Piña-Aguilar, Janet Lopez-Saucedo and Antonio Gutiérrez-Gutiérrez are scientists at the Instituto de Ciencias en Reproducción Humana Vida in León, Mexico; Richard Sheffield, Lilia I. Ruiz-Galaz, and Jose de J. Barroso-Padilla are scientists at the Parque Zoológico de León. In the following viewpoint, they report that scientists have already successfully cloned an extinct animal. They say that other conservation methods are also needed and that cloning alone cannot bring back viable populations of extinct animals. Nonetheless, they argue, cloning is a valuable resource for conservationists.

As you read, consider the following questions:

1. What happened to the cloned Pyrenean ibex female after it was born, according to the authors?

2. What figures do the authors use to show the crisis of extinction among mammals?

Raul E. Piña-Aguilar, Janet Lopez-Saucedo, Richard Sheffield, Lilia I. Ruiz-Galaz, Jose de J. Barroso-Padilla, and Antonio Gutiérrez-Gutiérrez, "Revival of Extinct Species Using Nuclear Transfer: Hope for the Mammoth, True for the Pyrenean Ibex, but Is It Time for 'Conservation Cloning'?," *Cloning and Stem Cells*, vol. 11, no. 3, September 14, 2009, pp. 341–345. Copyright © 2009 by Mary Ann Liebert, Inc. All rights reserved. Reproduced by permission.

3. What do the authors say is more important than bringing back extinct species?

Recent experiments in somatic cell nuclear transfer (SCNT) [a laboratory technique for creating a cloned embryo that uses an unfertilized egg from one animal and injects the genetic material to be cloned from another animal] and genomics are reviving with great force the hope for extinct animal "resurrections," a suggestion generated some years ago with the birth of Dolly [the first cloned sheep] and the announcement of the thylacine cloning project (also known as the Tasmanian tiger *Thylacinus cynocephalus*) in 1999 in Australia, which was based on a museum specimen [preserved] in alcohol. . . .

Reviving Extinct Species

These accomplishments are receiving tremendous media attention, and as the revival of an extinct species becomes more and more possible, public interest is increased. Furthermore, the scientific community is being given an important amount of coverage, such as the excellent article dedicated to mammoth revival, citing goals and challenges and a top 10 list of mammals to revive, including DNA preservation status and the availability of suitable surrogates for each species. . . .

However, extinct species resurrection is not a matter of hope; it is a reality. The birth of a Pyrenean ibex (*Capra pyrenaica pyrenaica*) using nuclear transfer techniques with somatic cells obtained from the last female ibex, was recently published. This female died in 2000, and with its death the Pyrenean ibex subspecies was extinct. This milestone achievement was accomplished by a multinational team from Spain, France, and Belgium, and they were led by Dr. Jose Folch of Zaragoza, Spain. The Pyrenean ibex cloning story started in 1999 with the capture of the last ibex in the National Ordesa Park in Huesca, Spain, for the purpose of taking skin biopsies, expanding *in vitro*, and freezing in liquid nitrogen. This goal was achieved, and cells were used for interspecific nuclear transfer experiments using domestic goat oocytes [egg cells]. The cloned embryos were transferred to pure Spanish ibex or hybrids (Spanish ibex male×domestic goat) recipients. Although the first experiments took place some years ago, and only two pregnancies were established without offspring, they were consequently considered a failure by public media sources. This new article reports the birth of a live Pyrenean ibex female from a hybrid goat mother, that unfortunately died minutes later from severe respiratory distress. Postmortem examination revealed an atelectasis [collapse of a lung] and the presence of a supplementary lobe in the left lung, which explained the cause of death. But nuclear DNA microsatellite analysis and mitochondrial DNA analysis confirmed that it was a true cloned offspring from the last Pyrenean ibex.

The subspecies cloning report will increase the flame for "resurrection hope" in extinct animals. In a recent article, [J.] Fulka mentioned about extinct animal cloning: "In the light of some other results . . . one must be cautious when saying: *this is impossible.*" Furthermore, together, these new results offer an opportunity for SCNT technology to be used in conservation efforts of critically endangered species and species close to extinction.

Extinct species resurrection is not a matter of hope; it is a reality.

Extinction Crisis

The rate of animal extinction and the number of species being threatened are overwhelming. Mammals are experiencing an extinction crisis, with almost one in four animals at risk of disappearing forever. According to the last assessment of the International Union for Conservation of Nature (IUCN) for threatened species, established in the IUCN Red List of Threatened Species (IUCN, 2008), there are 83 species or subspecies of mammals listed as extinct; 2 species of mammals being listed as extinct in the wild and 260 species of listed mammals as critically endangered of the approximately 5,400 worldwide species of mammals (6.38%). In addition to these species there are remaining categories of risk (endangered, vulnerable, or with deficient data). Based on these numbers and the fact that species survival is directly related with species reproduction capability, scientists have been proposing nuclear transfer technology as a tool in biological conservation even since the early history of reproductive cloning, and it is now being extensively reviewed.

However, until now SCNT has not had the potential to be considered as a true option for biological conservation efforts, because only isolated success has been obtained with wildlife species, such as the gaur, the mouflon, the African wildcat, the gray wolf, the red deer and the sand cat, and recently the Pyrenean ibex. A few offspring were born, and they died shortly after birth. This contrasts with the success obtained in domestic species such as bovines. Furthermore, for endangered species conservation purposes, it is indisputable that the best method of assisted reproduction is artificial insemination with frozen semen, making the role of SCNT for these purposes more difficult.

Mammals are experiencing an extinction crisis, with almost one in four animals at risk of disappearing forever.

The poor performance of nuclear transfer in wildlife is caused by many challenges and obstacles, including poor knowledge of species reproductive biology, lack of oocytes [eggs] for cytoplasts source (in most cases interspecific), and suitable embryo recipients of cloned embryos (also in most cases interspecific). In the case of mammoth revival and in addition to the above mentioned obstacles, cell nuclei with relative DNA integrity are needed—a difficult task because DNA sequencing of the mammoth has revealed that only 80% of its DNA corresponds to the actual mammoth, and the rest to other species.

The oocyte source for a mammoth can be Asian elephants (*Elephas maximus*) as it has the closest DNA sequence relation; however, the use of Asian elephants is near to impossible [because of its unique reproductive cycle]. Supposing a potential case of mammoth cloned embryo production using elephant oocytes, finding a suitable number of recipients is totally impossible; in the Association of Zoos and Aquariums (AZA) affiliated zoos, there exist only 220 females, and few are capable of breeding. . . . Furthermore, the principal barrier is that Asian elephants are an endangered species, and it is completely unethical to use these animals for cloning a mammoth, thus making the experiment a really poor potential for biological conservation and final success.

In the case of SCNT and other assisted reproduction techniques for biological conservation purposes, reproductive scientists and conservation biologists have a confrontation about their potential. This conflict was masterfully expressed by [W.V.] Holt and [R.E.] Lloyd (2009): ". . . there is also a perception problem about reproductive biology—the discipline is poorly understood by colleagues in the wildlife community. Reproduction is not even listed under 'topics of interest' in major journals devoted to biodiversity conservation. One reason for such benign disregard is that reproductive scientists are often seen as enamoured with using 'high-tech' assisted breeding methods. Conservation biologists traditionally have avoided technical solutions, fearing that reproductive technologies could divert funds from protecting habitats, while giving a false sense of security that species on the brink of extinction could be easily resurrected." However, in some cases, as in the black-footed ferret (*Mustela nigripes*), one of the

---

**Endangered or Extinct Species
That Are Candidates for Cloning**

Species	Species That Are Sources and Recipients of Eggs in the Cloning Process
Black-footed ferret (*Mustela nigripes*)	Domestic ferrets
Père David's deer (*Elaphurus davidianus*)	Red deer or Père David's deer hybrids
Riverine rabbit (*Bunolagus monticularis*)	Domestic rabbit
Red wolf (*Canis rufus*)	Domestic dogs / Gray wolves
African wild ass (*Equus africanus*)	Domestic donkey
Javan leopard (*Panthera pardus melas*)	Leopard subspecies hybrids
South China tiger (*Panthera tigris amoyensis*)	Domestic cat / Tiger subspecies hybrids
Visayan warty pig (*Sus cebifrons*)	Domestic pig

TAKEN FROM: Raul E. Piña-Aguilar et al., "Revival of Extinct Species Using Nuclear Transfer: Hope for the Mammoth, True for the Pyrenean Ibex, but Is It Time for 'Conservation Cloning'?," *Cloning and Stem Cells*, September 14, 2009, vol. 11, no. 3, pp. 342–345.

---

most endangered North American mammals, reproduction technologies have opened the opportunity for this species' survival, and also in other species there is a complete program of assisted reproductive technologies (ARTs) available including SCNT, as in the mouflon. These programs can be helpful for conservation and natural population genetic management.

The Pyrenean Ibex

Even though the biological community has rejected SCNT, we believe there might be a window of opportunity that would emend this rejection, for example, the use of the SCNT approach with species that are close to the brink of extinction, and those whose population status, geographical isolation, or complicated reproductive characteristics make it really difficult to use other assisted reproduction approaches. A good example of the previously mentioned is the Pyrenean ibex. At this time there only exist cryopreserved cells of the last female. Although Pyrenean ibex's SCNT will not restore the natural population, as it is close to impossible in any species, SCNT offers an opportunity to study and understand reproductive mechanisms while even helping to improve the knowledge of other species with more conservation potential such as other subspecies of the Spanish ibex (*Capra pyrenaica*).

Taking into account the mammals that are registered in the IUCN's red list, we chose a sample listing of potential mammals [see graphic], based on their particular characteristics, critical status, and/or availability of similar model; this would make SCNT a possible and successful approach for conservation and help rescue some mammals from extinction. This list does not include marine mammals, bats, or rodents; the latter might represent an excellent candidate, because SCNT in mice is more developed and has a better rate of success than in other species.

We have included on this list important regional cases such as the Mexican gray wolf (*Canis lupus baileyi*), historically distributed in Mexico and the United States, and now declared extinct in the wild in Mexico. It has been reintroduced in certain parts of New Mexico and Arizona where extinction in the wild has persisted for many years. The captive population has saved them from complete extinction. They are genetically well characterized, and conservation efforts are well developed based on binational programs involving zoos and wildlife reserves. Furthermore, the SCNT model for this subspecies can be considered optimal because gray wolves (*Canis lupus*) have been cloned with relatively great success using domestic dog oocytes and embryo recipients. And even better, the generic gray wolf can be used as an oocyte donor and embryo recipient, as it is not an endangered species. . . .

"Resurrection" of extinct animals is a dream of mankind.

It is also noteworthy to mention that it is improbable that using only one approach such as SCNT . . . , we will recover critical endangered populations. . . . The most effective measures are to reduce negative human influence on wildlife, [disseminate] conservation education to the general public, and involve [community] participation in conservation efforts. But it is nevertheless correct to say that every individual effort in our battle to conserve, propagate, and protect our wildlife is valid and most necessary.

"Resurrection" of extinct animals is a dream of mankind, nourished by fiction, as is the case of the legendary *Jurassic Park* film [a 1993 movie that imagined a park of dinosaur clones]. It inspired a complete generation of kids and scientists. It is also a dream of science that was recently inspired with the first revival of an extinct animal: the Pyrenean ibex. But it is of more importance to help conserve the living species that are close to being gone forever than bringing back extinct ones, but nevertheless, we should not restrict the proven benefits and potential of SCNT technology, one of the most powerful modern biological techniques that exist today in biological conservation.

Position Statement on the OIE Guidelines on Somatic Cell Nuclear Transfer in Production Livestock and Horses

International Coalition for Animal Welfare

The International Coalition for Animal Welfare (ICFAW)[1] is a coalition of nongovernmental animal welfare organizations from all over the world. In the following viewpoint, ICFAW argues that pregnancies involving clones are stressful to adult animal mothers and result in high mortality rates among cloned animal fetuses and infants. ICFAW also argues that cloned adult animals are unhealthy. Further, ICFAW maintains, cloning is used to perpetuate factory farming, which is cruel to animals. For all these reasons, ICFAW says, cloning should be discouraged.

As you read, consider the following questions:

1. According to ICFAW, what is large offspring syndrome, and how is it related to cloning?

---

[1] The member organisations of the International Coalition for Animal Welfare, representing more than 12 million individual supporters internationally, include: Compassion in World Farming, Eurogroup for Animals, the Humane Society of the United States and Humane Society International, the International Fund for Animal Welfare, the Japanese Farm Animal Welfare Initiative, the National Council of SPCAs, the Royal Society for the Prevention of Cruelty to Animals, RSPCA Australia, and the World Society for the Protection of Animals.

2. What are the range of factors that ICFAW says contributes to high rates of mortality and ill health for clones in the postnatal period?

3. Why will the cloning of high-yielding animals result in an increase of animal suffering, according to ICFAW?

OIE guidelines for somatic cell nuclear transfer in production livestock and horses appear in the report of the meeting of the OIE Terrestrial Animal Health Commission on 10–14 March 2008.

The International Coalition for Animal Welfare (ICFAW) believes that the OIE guidelines give insufficient attention to the scientific literature that establishes that cloning entails serious health and welfare problems for animal clones and their surrogate dams. ICFAW respectfully urges the OIE to give further consideration to its guidelines as we think that they should give greater weight to these health and welfare concerns.

Somatic cell nuclear transfer is a method of cloning, i.e., of artificial reproduction used to produce a genetically identical or almost identical copy of an individual animal. Animal health and welfare problems arise due to:

- The invasive techniques required to produce a clone

- The suffering of surrogate dams who carry cloned foetuses

- High levels of ill health and mortality in the early stages of life of cloned animals.

A paper published in the OIE's *Revue Scientifique et Technique* has identified the serious problems involved in cloning:

[A]t present it is an inefficient process: In cattle, only around 6% of the embryos transferred to the reproductive tracts of recipient cows result in healthy, long-term surviving clones. Of concern are the high losses throughout gestation, during birth and in the post-natal period through to adulthood. Many of the pregnancy losses relate to failure of the placenta to develop and function correctly. Placental dysfunction may also have an adverse influence on post-natal health.[2]

The paper added that the incidence of gastrointestinal, umbilical and respiratory infections is increased in cloned livestock.

[A]t present [cloning] is an inefficient process: In cattle, only around 6% of the embryos transferred to the reproductive tracts of recipient cows result in healthy, long-term surviving clones.

Ian Wilmut, who led the team that cloned Dolly the sheep, is quoted as saying: "The widespread problems associated with clones has [*sic*] led to questions as to whether any clone was entirely normal. . . . There is abundant evidence that cloning can and does go wrong. . . ."[3]

Scientific Opinion of the European Food Safety Authority

In July 2008 the European Food Safety Authority (EFSA) published a Scientific Opinion.[4] This points out that:

- There is an increased proportion of pregnancy failure and disorders in surrogate dams of cloned embryos.

---

[2] Wells DN. 2005. Animal cloning: problems and prospects. Revue Scientifique et Technique (International Office of Epizootics) 24(1):251-64.

[3] Leake J. 2002. Gene defects emerge in all animal clones. The Sunday Times (UK), April 28.

[4] European Food Safety Authority, 2008. Scientific opinion on food safety, animal health and welfare, and environmental impact of animals derived from cloning by somatic cell nuclear transfer (SCNT) and their offspring and products obtained from those animals (Question No EFSA-Q-2007-092). The EFSA Journal (2008) 767, 1-49.

- These disorders and the large size of clones make Caesareans more frequent in cattle-carrying clones than in conventional pregnancies.

- The health and welfare of a significant proportion of cloned animals have been found to be adversely affected, often severely and with a fatal outcome.

- The welfare of both the surrogate dam and the clone can be affected by adverse health outcomes.

Opinion of the European Group on Ethics

In January 2008 the European Group on Ethics in Science and New Technologies to the European Commission (EGE) published an opinion on cloning.[5] This concluded that "considering the current level of suffering and health problems of surrogate dams and animal clones, the EGE has doubts as to whether cloning animals for food supply is ethically justified". The EGE added that it "does not see convincing arguments to justify the production of food from clones and their offspring".

A substantial proportion of clones die during pregnancy.

Invasive Reproduction Techniques

Once a cloned embryo has been produced, it is implanted into a surrogate mother who carries out the pregnancy. In pigs the transfer of the embryo into the surrogate mother is performed by a surgical procedure. In cattle embryo transfer is sufficiently stressful that UK legislation requires a general or epidural anaesthetic.

Suffering of Surrogate Dams

Large offspring syndrome is common in cloned calves and lambs. Cloned calves are often 25% heavier than normal which

---

[5] The European Group on Ethics in Science and New Technologies to the European Commission. 2008. Ethical aspects of animal cloning for food supply, Opinion No. 23, January 16.

leads to painful births for the surrogate mothers and to most deliveries being performed by Caesarean section. The EFSA opinion points out that "dystocia [abnormal or difficult birth] carries the risk of unrelieved 'extra' pain during birth due to the large offspring. If the dam has to have a Caesarean section then that itself carries the risk of pain and anxiety due to the procedures involved, including a failure to provide adequate post-operative pain relief. If the Caesarean section is not planned then there is the added burden of both the pain of dystocia and the Caesarean section."

Mortality During Pregnancy

A substantial proportion of clones die during pregnancy, often from placental and foetal abnormalities, or are stillborn. The EFSA opinion states that there is a high rate of pregnancy failure in surrogate dams and that this has been linked to abnormal and/or poorly developed placental formation. Such placental defects have been associated with early embryonic loss, abortions, stillbirths, dystocia and pre- and post-natal deaths. A 2007 study reported that 25% of cows pregnant with cloned embryos at day 120 of gestation develop hydroallantois (abnormal fluid accumulation in the allantoic cavity of the placenta) and their pregnancies have to be terminated.[6]

Inefficiency and Wastage of Life

Cloning is a wasteful process. A 2004 paper reported that only 13% of cloned calf embryos implanted into surrogate dams results in calves delivered at full term.[7] A 2003 review of clon-

[6] Laible, G. and Wells, D. N. 2007. Recent advances and future options for New Zealand agriculture derived from animal cloning and transgenics. *New Zealand Journal of Agriculture Research* 50: 103-124.

[7] Wells, D.N. 2004. *The integration of cloning by nuclear transfer in the conservation of animal genetic resources.* In: Simm G et al.(Eds). Farm animal genetic resources. British Association of Animal Science, pp 223-241.

The Morality of Cloning Pets

Is it people's personal business how they spend their money on pets? Whether they want to try cloning to re-create a loved pet's genotype? Not so, says . . . Wayne Pacelle [of the Humane Society of the United States], who called the Missyplicity Project [devoted to cloning a pet dog] "perfectly awful" when so many dogs get euthanized while waiting to be adopted. Representing People for the Ethical Treatment of Animals (PETA), Michael W. Fox, the well-known animal rights advocate and veterinarian, says, "Dog cloning is a sentimental self-indulgence for those who can afford it."

Fox also objects to the sixty-one female dogs that supply the eggs into which nuclei of Missy are injected to create embryonic clones of Missy. "Those dogs in the Missyplicity dog colony are hormonally manipulated to ovulate faster than normal. Eventually, that's going to wear them down to the point that they'll develop diseases earlier and start dying sooner. We've only recently gotten down from the trees, and we're already playing God. We need to think about our responsibilities to animals."

Gregory E. Pence, Cloning After Dolly: Who's Still Afraid?
Lanham, MD: Rowman & Littlefield, 2004, pp. 35–36.

ing procedures reported that less than 5% of all cloned embryos transferred into recipient cows have survived.[8]

A recent paper refers to the cloning process as "inefficient and highly prone to epigenetic errors".[9] Due to the low efficiency of the cloning process, a high number of surrogate dams are required to produce a low number of clones.

[8] Oback B and Wells DN. 2003. Cloning cattle. Cloning and Stem Cells 5(4):243-56.

[9] As 5.

Perinatal Problems and Post-Natal Mortality of Cloned Animals

Many clones die in the early stages of life. In a 2007 paper researchers from the U.S. Food and Drug Administration noted "that perinatal calf and lamb clones have an increased risk of death and birth defects".[10] The EFSA opinion states that changes observed in late gestation in clones from cattle and sheep give rise to an increase in perinatal deaths, excess foetal size, abnormal placental development, enlarged internal organs, increased susceptibility to disease, sudden death, reluctance to suckle and difficulty in breathing and standing.

The EGE opinion states that around 20% of calves do not survive the first 24 hours after birth, and an additional 15% die before weaning. Similar findings were reported by Panarace et al. in 2007 who summarised five years of commercial experience of cloning cattle in three countries.[11] On average 42% of cattle clones died between delivery and 150 days of life and the most common abnormalities were enlarged umbilical cords (37%), respiratory problems (19%), depressed or weak calves displayed by prolonged recumbency (20%) and contracted flexor tendons (21%).

The high rates of mortality and ill health are due to a range of factors including:

- Immune deficiencies

- Respiratory problems

- Cardiovascular failure

- Liver failure

---

[10] Rudenko L and Matheson JC. 2007. The U.S. FDA and animal cloning: risk and regulatory approach. Theriogenology 67(1):198-206.

[11] Panarace, M., Aguero, J. I., Garrote, M., Jauregui, G., Segovia, A., Cane, L., Gutierrez, J., Marfil, M., Rigali, F., Pugliese, M., Young, S., Lagioia, J., Garnil, C., Forte Pontes, J. E., Ereno Junio, J. C., Mower, S. and Medina, M. 2007. How healthy are clones and their progeny: 5 years of field experience. *Theriogenology* 67 (1): 142-51.

- Kidney abnormalities

- Musculoskeletal abnormalities.

Examples of these problems can be seen in two cases of piglet mortality. In 2003 three cloned pigs out of a group of four died of heart attacks before the age of six months; the fourth had died a few days after birth. In another case, of seven cloned piglets, two died shortly after birth from breathing problems and a third died after 17 days from heart failure. Of the survivors, one had heart and lung abnormalities, one had eye and ear abnormalities and one had a leg joint abnormality.

Loi et al. published an account of the death of a group of cloned lambs in 2006. Out of 93 clones transferred to surrogate dams, only 12 reached full-term development. Of these twelve, three were stillborn and five died within 24 hours, displaying degenerative lesions in the liver and kidneys. Another two died 24 hours after birth from respiratory distress syndrome. The final two cloned lambs showed respiratory dysfunction and died at around one month due to a bacterial complication.[12]

In 2003 three cloned pigs out of a group of four died of heart attacks before the age of six months; the fourth had died a few days after birth.

A study undertaken at the US Department of Agriculture and published in October 2005 suggested that clones may be born with defective immune systems. The finding could explain why clones often die from infections soon after birth.[13]

[12] Loi, P., Clinton M., Vackova I., Fulka J Jr., Feil R., Palmieri C., Della Salda L., Ptak G., 2006. Placental abnormalities associated with post-natal mortality in sheep somatic cell clones. *Theriogenology* 65 (2006) 1110-1121.

[13] Carroll, J.A., Bart Carter, D., Korte, S.C., Prather, R.S. 2005. Evaluation of the acute phase response in cloned pigs following a lipopolysaccharide challenge. *Domestic Animal Endocrinology* 29: 564-572.

Team leader Jeff Carroll says: "I've looked at the immune response of hundreds of young pigs and I've never seen anything that low until I looked at a clone".[14]

Some abnormalities may not show up until later in life. Writing in the OIE *Revue Scientifique et Technique* a leading cloning scientist pointed out that the development of musculoskeletal problems, such as chronic lameness and severely contracted flexor tendons, in these high-production animals "emphasises the point that any underlying frailties in cloned animals may not be fully revealed until the animals are stressed in some manner."[15] Wells et al. found that the most common cause of death of cattle they cloned were late-developing musculoskeletal problems so severe that the cows needed to be euthanized.[16]

Likely Suffering of Cloned Animals and Their Offspring When Raised On-Farm

To correctly assess the long-term impact of cloning on the welfare of cattle and pigs, ICFAW believes that it is important to consider the ways in which cloning is likely to be used within the livestock sector. The likelihood is that cloning will be used to multiply the highest yielding cows and fastest growing pigs. Yet research shows that these animals are likely to suffer from metabolic and physiological disorders associated with fast growth and excessive muscle or udder development.

Traditional selective breeding has already led to major health problems for such animals. Fast growing pigs suffer from leg disorders and cardiovascular malfunction[17] and high

---

[14] New Scientist News Staff. 2004. The problem with clones. *New Scientist* 06/11/04, page 20.

[15] As 1.

[16] Wells DN, Forsyth JT, McMillan V, and Oback B. 2004. The health of somatic cell cloned cattle and their offspring. Cloning and Stem Cells 6(2):101-10.

[17] Scientific Opinion of the Panel on Animal Health and Welfare on a request from the Commission on Animal health and welfare in fattening pigs in relation to housing and husbandry. *The EFSA Journal* (2007) 564, 1-14.

yielding cattle from lameness, mastitis and premature culling; the cloning of the most fast growing and high yielding animals will lead to an even higher proportion of animals suffering from the same health and welfare problems.

ICFAW believes that cloning of farm animals is taking us in the wrong direction—towards perpetuating industrial farming when all other societal trends point towards sustainable farming and respect for animals as sentient beings.

Increased Susceptibility to Disease

A herd of cloned animals or their offspring will have less genetic diversity than a conventional herd and so will have increased vulnerability to a disease challenge. The EGE said that the use of a limited number of breeding lines in intensive animal farming may affect the biodiversity of farm animals and create inbreeding problems.

It is claimed that it will be mainly offspring of clones that will be used on-farm, with the clones themselves being used for breeding. It is further argued that the offspring of clones do not suffer from unusual health problems. However, few studies have been carried out on the health of the offspring of clones and none have been reported on their welfare. Moreover, even if the offspring of clones are as healthy as normal animals, the fact remains that the clones themselves and their surrogate dams often experience substantial suffering and health problems.

ICFAW believes that cloning of farm animals is taking us in the wrong direction—towards perpetuating industrial farming when all other societal trends point towards sustainable farming and respect for animals as sentient beings.

Chinese Scientists Seek to Use Genetically Modified Pigs to Treat Human Illnesses

Oxford Journals

Oxford Journals is a division of Oxford University Press. The following viewpoint reports that Chinese scientists have taken important steps forward in genetically engineering pigs to provide organs for transplants to humans. According to the author, the advances could also be used to create models in pigs to study human genetic diseases or to increase the pigs' resistance to disease. The author concludes that this is an important advancement that could greatly benefit human and animal health.

As you read, consider the following questions:

1. What are somatic cells, according to the viewpoint?
2. What does Dr. Xiao say would have to be modified in pigs in order to make pig organs compatible with humans?
3. How does Dr. Xiao believe his discovery could improve animal farming?

Scientists have managed to induce cells from pigs to transform into pluripotent stem cells—cells that, like embryonic stem cells, are capable of developing into any type of cell in

Oxford Journals, "World First: Chinese Scientists Create Pig Stem Cells. Discovery Has Far-Reaching Implications for Animal and Human Health," June 3, 2009. www.oxford journals.org.

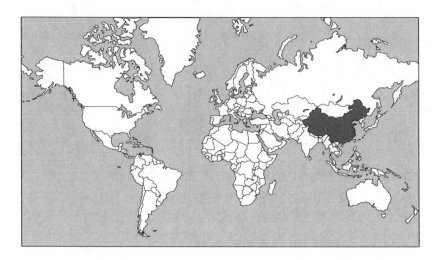

the body. It is the first time in the world that this has been achieved using somatic cells (cells that are not sperm or egg cells) from any animal with hooves (known as ungulates).

The implications of this achievement are far-reaching; the research could open the way to creating models for human genetic diseases, genetically engineering animals for organ transplants for humans, and for developing pigs that are resistant to diseases such as swine flu.

The work is the first research paper to be published online today (Wednesday 3 June) in the newly launched *Journal of Molecular Cell Biology*.[1]

Dr Lei Xiao, who led the research, said: "To date, many efforts have been made to establish ungulate pluripotent embryonic stem cells from early embryos without success. This is the first report in the world of the creation of domesticated ungulate pluripotent stem cells. Therefore, it is entirely new, very important and has a number of applications for both human and animal health."

---

[1] Generation of pig induced pluripotent stem cells with a drug-inducible system. *Journal of Molecular Cell Biology*. doi:10.1093/jmcb/jmp003. A pdf of the full research paper is available at http://www.oxfordjournals.org/our_journals/jmcb/mjp003.pdf.

Dr Xiao, who heads the stem cell lab at the Shanghai Institute of Biochemistry and Cell Biology (Shanghai, China), and colleagues succeeded in generating induced pluripotent stem cells by using transcription factors to reprogramme cells taken from a pig's ear and bone marrow. After the cocktail of reprogramming factors had been introduced into the cells via a virus, the cells changed and developed in the laboratory into colonies of embryonic-like stem cells. Further tests confirmed that they were, in fact, stem cells capable of differentiating into the cell types that make up the three layers in an embryo—endoderm, mesoderm and ectoderm—a quality that all embryonic stem cells have. The information gained from successfully inducing pluripotent stem cells (iPS cells) means that it will be much easier for researchers to go on to develop embryonic stem cells (ES cells) that originate from pig or other ungulate embryos.

"It is entirely new, very important and has a number of applications for both human and animal health."

Dr Xiao said: "Pig pluripotent stem cells would be useful in a number of ways, such as precisely engineering transgenic animals for organ transplantation therapies. The pig species is significantly similar to humans in its form and function, and the organ dimensions are largely similar to human organs. We could use embryonic stem cells or induced stem cells to modify the immune-related genes in the pig to make the pig organ compatible to the human immune system. Then we could use these pigs as organ donors to provide organs for patients that won't trigger an adverse reaction from the patient's own immune system.

"Pig pluripotent stem cell lines could also be used to create models for human genetic diseases. Many human diseases, such as diabetes, are caused by a disorder of gene expression. We could modify the pig gene in the stem cells and generate pigs carrying the same gene disorder so that they would have a similar syndrome to that seen in human patients. Then it would be possible to use the pig model to develop therapies to treat the disease.

"We could use these pigs as organ donors to provide organs for patients that won't trigger an adverse reaction from the patient's own immune system."

"To combat swine flu, for instance, we could make a precise, gene-modified pig to improve the animal's resistance to the disease. We would do this by first, finding a gene that has anti–swine flu activity, or inhibits the proliferation of the swine flu virus; second, we can introduce this gene to the pig via pluripotent stem cells—a process known as gene 'knock-in'. Alternatively, because the swine flu virus needs to bind with a receptor on the cell membrane of the pig to enter the cells and proliferate, we could knock out this receptor in the pig via gene targeting in the pig induced pluripotent stem cell. If the receptor is missing, the virus will not infect the pig."

In addition to medical applications for pigs and humans, Dr Xiao said his discovery could be used to improve animal farming, not only by making the pigs healthier, but also by modifying the growth-related genes to change and improve the way the pigs grow.

However, Dr Xiao warned that it could take several years before some of the potential medical applications of his research could be used in the clinic.

The next stage of his research is to use the pig iPS cells to generate gene-modified pigs that could provide organs for patients, improve the pig species or be used for disease resistance. The modified animals would be either "knock-in" pigs where the iPS or ES cells have been used to transfer an additional bit of genetic material (such as a piece of human DNA) into the pig's genome, or "knock-out" pigs where the technology is used to prevent a particular gene functioning.

Commenting on the study, the journal's editor in chief, Professor Dangsheng Li, said: "This research is very exciting because it represents the first rigorous demonstration of the establishment of pluripotent stem cell in ungulate species, which will open up interesting opportunities for creating precise, gene-modified animals for research, therapeutic and agricultural purposes."

Periodical and Internet Sources Bibliography

The following articles have been selected to supplement the diverse views presented in this chapter.

Richard Alleyne	"Animal to Human Organ Transplants Come Closer After GM Pig Breakthrough," *Telegraph*, June 3, 2009.
British Society of Animal Science	"Genetic Modification of Farm Animals," 2012. www.bsas.org.uk.
Steve Connor	"A Giant Leap into the Unknown: GM Salmon That Grows and Grows," *Independent*, September 22, 2010.
Richard Gray and Robert Dobson	"Extinct Ibex Is Resurrected by Cloning," *Telegraph*, January 31, 2009.
Tom Mueller	"Recipe for a Resurrection," *National Geographic*, May 2009.
Sara Novak	"GM Salmon No Longer Dead in the Water Thanks to USDA Funding," Treehugger, November 12, 2011. www.treehugger.com.
Sean Poulter	"Clone Farming Would Introduce Cruelty on a Massive Scale, Say Animal Welfare Groups," *Daily Mail*, November 26, 2010.
Abbie Smith	"Animal-Human Organ Transplant Trials Expected in 2013," *Healthcare Global*, October 21, 2011.
Emily Sohn	"Is Genetically Modified Salmon Safe?," DiscoveryNews, September 10, 2010. http://news.discovery.com.
Bryan Walsh	"Frankenfish: Is GM Salmon a Vital Part of Our Future?," *Time*, July 12, 2011.

CHAPTER 4

Genetic Engineering in Humans

Genetic Testing Will Help Many with Dangerous Diseases

Claudia Kalb

Claudia Kalb is a senior writer at Newsweek, *focusing on health and medical issues. In the following viewpoint, she reports on genetic advances that have made it possible to detect many dangerous illnesses. She also says that in some cases, genetic testing can help parents anticipate and treat health problems in their children, or even screen embryos for dangerous genetic disorders. Kalb says that scientists hope to use genetic testing to find cures for more common illnesses, such as heart disease. She notes that such cures may never happen but concludes that genetic testing is an exciting medical advance that may produce great benefits in the future.*

As you read, consider the following questions:

1. According to Kalb, what is isovaleric acidemia, and how can genetic testing help in treating it?
2. Why does Kalb say that people at risk of Huntington's disease often do not take the genetic test to determine if they have the illness?
3. What is the HapMap, according to Kalb?

The year is 1895 and Pauline Gross, a young seamstress, is scared. Gross knows nothing about the double helix or the human genome project [that sequenced the human genetic code]—such medical triumphs are far in the future. But she does know about a nasty disease called cancer, and it's running through her family. "I'm healthy now," she reportedly confides to Dr. Aldred Warthin, a pathologist at the University of Michigan, "but I fully expect to die an early death."

Changing Medicine

At the time, Gross's prediction (she did indeed die young of cancer) was based solely on observation: Family members had succumbed to colon and endometrial cancer; she would, too. Today, more than 100 years later, Gross's relatives have a much more clinical option: genetic testing. With a simple blood test, they can peer into their own DNA, learning—while still perfectly healthy—whether they carry a hereditary gene mutation that has dogged their family for decades and puts them at serious risk. Ami McKay, 38, whose great-grandmother Tilly was Gross's sister, decided she wanted to know for her children's sake. In 2002, the answer came back: positive. "It changes who you are," says McKay.

Genetic testing is changing medicine, too. Three years after scientists announced they had sequenced the human genome, new knowledge about how our genes affect our health is transforming the way diseases are understood, diagnosed, treated—and even predicted. Today gene tests are available for more than 1,300 diseases, including cystic fibrosis and hemophilia. And now, as genetic screening gets cheaper and faster, researchers are hunting down the biological underpinnings of more complex disorders that involve multiple genes—big, rampaging illnesses that strike millions of Americans every year. On the list: type 2 diabetes, Alzheimer's [disease], heart disease and depression. If the scientists are right, genetic tests for some of these diseases could be available by 2010. Testing positive doesn't guarantee that you'll get the illness, but it does help determine your risk. "We are on the leading edge of a genuine revolution," says Dr. Francis Collins, head of the National Human Genome Research Institute.

Genetic testing today starts at the earliest stages of life. Couples planning to have children can be screened prior to conception to see if they are carriers of genetic diseases; prenatal tests are offered during pregnancy, and states now screen newborns for as many as 29 conditions, the majority of them genetic disorders. For Jana and Tom Monaco, of Woodbridge, Va., early testing has made an enormous difference in the lives of their children. Their journey began in 2001, when their seemingly healthy third child, 3-year-old Stephen, developed a life-threatening stomach virus that led to severe brain damage. His diagnosis: a rare but treatable disease called isovaleric acidemia (IVA), marked by the body's inability to metabolize an amino acid found in dietary protein. Unknowingly, Jana and her husband were carriers of the disease, and at the time, IVA was not included in newborn screening. The Monacos had no warning whatsoever.

Today gene tests are available for more than 1,300 diseases, including cystic fibrosis and hemophilia.

Early Warning

Not so when Jana got pregnant again. Her daughter, Caroline, was tested by amnio [amniocentesis, a test performed on a fetus] while still in the womb. Knowing Caroline had the mutation, doctors were able to administer medication the day she was born. And the Monacos were prepared to monitor her diet immediately to keep her healthy. Today Stephen, 9, is unable to walk, talk or feed himself. Caroline, meanwhile, is an active, healthy 4-year-old. Genetic testing, says Jana, "gives Caroline the future that Stephen didn't get to have."

The future is what drives many adults to the clinic. The gene tests currently offered for certain diseases, like breast and colon cancer, affect only a small percentage of total cases. Inherited mutations, including BRCA1 and 2, contribute to just 5 to 10 percent of all breast cancers, and the main gene variants involved in colon cancer account for 3 to 5 percent of diagnoses. But the impact on a single life can be huge. The key: being able to do something to ward off disease. "Genetic testing offers us profound insight," says Dr. Stephen Gruber, of the University of Michigan. "But it has to be balanced with our ability to care for these patients."

Caroline ... was tested ... while still in the womb. Knowing Caroline had the mutation, doctors were able to administer medication the day she was born.

Ami McKay now has an annual colonoscopy. Another kind of genetically driven colon cancer, familial polyposis, is treated by removing the colon. The risk of breast and ovarian cancers in people with BRCA mutations can be reduced by frequent screening and radical surgery, too. Having healthy breasts or ovaries removed isn't easy, but the payoff—an end to constant anxiety and a preemptive strike at disease—can be well worth it. "Most women I've met who've had prophylactic surgery are glad they made the choice even if they're unhappy they were put in that position," says Sue Friedman, a breast-cancer survivor and head of FORCE [Facing Our Risk of Cancer], an advocacy and support group focused on hereditary cancers. "It's a double-edged sword."

Genetic testing, exciting as it may seem, isn't always the answer. When Wendy Uhlmann, a genetic counselor at the University of Michigan, teaches medical students, she flashes two slides on a screen side by side. One says ignorance is bliss. The other: Knowledge is power. That's because the value of testing becomes especially murky—and ethically complicated

—when there is no way to prevent or treat disease, as in the case of early-onset Alzheimer's [that causes memory loss and eventually death], which often strikes before the age of 50, or Huntington's [disease].

Today only about 5 percent of people who are at risk for Huntington's—which is caused by a single gene and leads to a progressive loss of physical control and mental acuity—take the test. Many are worried that genetic testing will put their health insurance or job security in jeopardy. While there have been few documented cases of discrimination, nobody can say for sure what will happen as more disease genes are discovered and more Americans sign on for predictive testing. States have a patchwork of regulations in place, but what needs to happen now, experts say, is for Congress to pass the Genetic Information Nondiscrimination Act, which would put a federal stamp of approval on keeping genetic information safe.

For Shana Martin, 26, of Madison, Wis., the decision not to get tested is far more personal. Shana grew up watching her mother, Deborah, battle Huntington's. Now a fitness instructor (and the current world champion in logrolling, no less), Shana is young, strong, healthy—and not interested in opening her genetic Pandora's box. "I don't know how well I'd handle a positive result, and with how happy I am right now, that would just put a real shadow over my life," she says. "I'm much more comfortable with it being an unknown."

Ignorance or Knowledge

Some people, however, can't live with uncertainty. Uhlmann's patient Stephanie Vogt knew Huntington's ran in her family— her paternal grandfather and his three brothers all died of complications of the disease—and she wanted to find out where she stood. "As soon as I found out there was a test, I just had to do it," she says. In August 2000, after comprehensive genetic counseling, Stephanie, her sister, Victoria, and

The Human Genome Project

Completed in 2003, the Human Genome Project (HGP) was a 13-year project coordinated by the U.S. Department of Energy and the National Institutes of Health. During the early years of the HGP, the Wellcome Trust (U.K.) became a major partner; additional contributions came from Japan, France, Germany, China, and others.

Project goals were to

- *identify* all the approximately 20,000–25,000 genes in human DNA,

- *determine* the sequences of the 3 billion chemical base pairs that make up human DNA,

- *store* this information in databases,

- *improve* tools for data analysis,

- *transfer* related technologies to the private sector, and

- *address* the ethical, legal, and social issues (ELSI) that may arise from the project.

Though the HGP is finished, analyses of the data will continue for many years.

OakRidge National Laboratory,
"Human Genome Project Information,"
July 25, 2011. www.ornl.gov.

their mother, Gayle Smith, learned her results: positive. "It was like a scene out of *The Matrix* [film], where everything freezes and starts again," says Stephanie, now 35 and single. Victoria, 36, who has since tested negative, says she hopes to care for her sister down the road. She also prays for a cure. Knowing isn't always easy. On good days Stephanie feels empowered; on bad days she's frightened. "But most of the time," she says, "I'm comfortable with the fact that I have the knowledge."

It's not just their own health that people care about. There is also the desire to prune disease from the family tree. Today, using a scientific advance called preimplantation genetic diagnosis (PGD), couples can create embryos through standard fertility methods, then screen them for genetic disorders, selecting only those that are mutation-free for implantation. The practice is expensive (in the tens of thousands of dollars) and not widespread, but a recent survey of fertility clinics by the Genetics and Public Policy Center found that 28 percent have used PGD to help couples avoid diseases that strike in adulthood, like breast cancer and Huntington's. Kari and Tim Baker knew they had to give it a try. Kari's grandfather died of Huntington's, and her mother was diagnosed in 1999. Kari, a board member of the Huntington's Disease Society of America, wanted to spare her kids. Twins Brooklyn and Levi are now vibrant 2 1/2-year-olds who will never have to worry. "There's great joy and peace in knowing we did everything we could to not pass this on," says Tim.

Testing is just one piece of the genomic revolution. A major goal is to create new sophisticated therapies that home in on a disease's biological glitch, then fix the problem. Already, genes are helping to predict a patient's response to existing medications. A prime example in this field of pharmacogenetics, says Dr. Wylie Burke of the University of Washington, is a variant of a gene called TPMT, which can lead to life-threatening reactions to certain doses of chemotherapy. A genetic test can guide safe and appropriate treatment. Two genes have been identified that influence a person's response to the anti-blood-clotting drug warfarin. And scientists are uncovering genetic differences in the way people respond to other widely used medications, like antidepressants.

Knowing a patient's genotype, or genetic profile, may also help researchers uncover new preventive therapies for intractable diseases. At Johns Hopkins University School of Medicine, Dr. Christopher Ross has tested several compounds shown to slow the progression of Huntington's in mice. Now he wants to test them in people who are positive for the Huntington's mutation but have not developed symptoms—a novel approach to clinical drug trials, which almost always involve sick people seeking cures. "We're using genetics to move from treating the disease after it happens," he says, "to preventing the worst symptoms of the disease before it happens."

"There's great joy and peace in knowing we did every-thing we could to not pass this [Huntington's disease] on," says Tim.

The HapMap

Early on, the targets of genetic medicine were rare, single-gene disorders, like sickle-cell anemia and Tay-Sachs [disease]. Now it's time for the big guns—genetically complex but common conditions like heart disease. A number of genes have already been linked to such illnesses, but many more are at work. The human genome project, which defines the 99.9 percent of DNA we all have in common, was the starting point. Act II: the "HapMap" [International HapMap Project]—a genetic atlas completed last year [2005] that zeroes in on the .1 percent of DNA that differs among individuals. The HapMap is proving to be a boon to scientists, allowing them to scan whole chunks of DNA, rather than single genes, to isolate mutations responsible for disease. Already, the HapMap has helped scientists uncover several gene variations that contribute to macular degeneration, the leading cause of vision loss in older people. At Harvard, Dr. Rudolph Tanzi is using the HapMap to track down gene mutations that cause the common, late-onset form of Alzheimer's, which could strike as many as 16 million Americans by the year 2050. Tanzi's work is funded by the Cure Alzheimer's Fund, a nonprofit that is investing $3 million to unravel the Alzheimer's genome, which it hopes to complete by the summer of 2008. Tanzi says a prototype genetic chip to test for the disease could be available within five years. Dr. Eric Topol, of Case Western Reserve University, is hunting down genes that predispose people to heart attacks.

Private companies, interested in developing drug therapies, are investing in DNA as well. In Iceland, deCODE Genetics has pinpointed a gene mutation for type 2 diabetes called TCF7L2. One copy of the mutation increases an individual's risk by 40 percent, two copies by 140 percent, says CEO Kári Stefánsson. Stefánsson says he expects a genetic test will be available as early as next year. And a joint effort by NIH [National Institutes of Health] and Pfizer, announced earlier this year, is searching for genes for a host of diseases, including schizophrenia, bipolar disease and severe depression.

It's hard not to get excited about the future, especially when you consider the medical competition now under way.

As science advances, business follows. Today genetic testing usually takes place in specialized clinics, where patients undergo thorough counseling both before and after testing so that they—and other family members—understand the emotional and practical implications that might arise. But do-it-yourself online testing companies, advertised directly to consumers, are springing up on the Internet. Ryan Phelan, CEO of DNA Direct, founded in 2004, says her site provides a "virtual genetics clinic," making testing as easy as sending in a cheek swab. (Cost: anywhere from $200 to $3,300.) DNA Direct provides counseling and does not sell remedies after results are in. But other companies are not so scrupulous, marketing tests that have little to no scientific validity, then pushing products as therapy. Critics say they need more oversight. "What you have here," says Dr. Adam Wolfberg, of Tufts-New England Medical Center, "is a real blurring of the lines between medical testing and product marketing."

Scientific revolutions must be tempered by reality. Genes aren't the only factors involved in complex diseases—lifestyle and environmental influences, such as diet or smoking, are too. And predictions about new tests and treatments may not come to pass as fast as researchers hope—they may not come at all. Still, it's hard not to get excited about the future, especially when you consider the medical competition now under way: NIH has challenged researchers to come up with a method, within the next 10 years, to sequence a single human genome for $1,000 (today's cost: $5 million to $10 million). Assuming it works, one day not too far in the future, each of us will go to the doc, hand over our blood and get back our personalized biological blueprints. "It's an astounding curve to be riding," says Collins. Hold on to your DNA.

Designer Babies, Stem Cells, and the Market for Genetics: The Limits of the Assisted Human Reproduction Act

Samantha King

Samantha King is an associate professor at Queen's University's School of Kinesiology and Health Studies and Women's Studies. In the following viewpoint, she notes that Canada has passed some helpful laws regulating genetic testing and fertility treatments. However, she says much more needs to be done to address the growth of the fertility industry and the dangers, particularly to women, of the industry's pursuit of perfect babies. In particular, she argues that society is too quick to terminate the pregnancies of babies with disabilities.

As you read, consider the following questions:

1. According to King, why is the Canadian act (the AHRA) a relatively progressive piece of legislation?

2. What does King say that prenatal technologies such as genetic screening encourage parents to do?

3. For what kinds of cloning does Geron hold the patent, according to King?

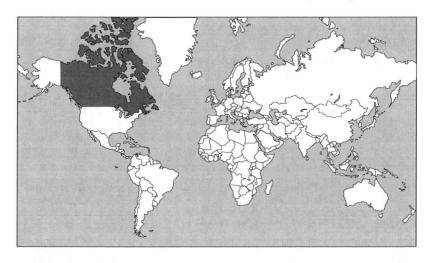

Hailed by liberal activists and policy makers as one of the most significant pieces of legislation worldwide to address human genetic and reproductive technologies, Bill C-6, *An Act Respecting [Assisted] Human Reproduction and Related Research* (popularly known as the Assisted Human Reproduction Act, or the AHRA), was approved by the Canadian senate on March 11, 2004. The act grew out of the Royal Commission on [New] Reproductive Technologies, which was established by the federal government in 1989. Its passing marked the formal end to a long and arduous consultative and legislative process that spawned three previously unsuccessful attempts to create a law governing human genetic and reproductive technologies (HGRTs).

In practice, however, the act is yet to be implemented and discussion about how to regulate the technologies in question is far from over. As these deliberations continue, there is a vital need to acknowledge feminist concerns about the cultural-commercial preoccupation with the production of perfect babies, a preoccupation that has, in many respects, become a routinized aspect of reproductive health care. Discourse on the act has largely skirted this issue and, with concern about the embryo front and centre, women's bodies have become all but invisible. Moreover, in the context of the unprecedented control now exercised by a supranational biotechnology industry over the development and commercialization of human genetic and reproductive technologies, it behooves us to recognize the limits of national law in facing the social and economic challenges presented by new HGRTs.

The most visible emblem of the ongoing tension that characterizes discussions about assisted human reproduction is the new government agency charged with developing and overseeing regulations and monitoring the fertility clinics and research facilities whose activities involve human gametes or embryos. The Assisted Human Reproduction Canada was formally established in January 2006, but it took until December 2007 for Prime Minister Stephen Harper to name appointees to its board, provoking charges on the part of women's health campaigners that the AHRA is merely a "paper dragon" (Lippman & Nisker, 2006). When the names of the board members were announced, moreover, critics from the fertility, stem cell research, and medical ethics communities cried foul, claiming that the panel is stacked with "social conservatives" (Brennan, 2007).

A recent article in the *Globe and Mail* ("Canada: Destination for Infertile Couples," Gazze 2007) draws attention to the degree to which the fertility industry continues to grow, apparently unfettered, in the face of inaction and political conflict. According to the article's author, Mary Gazze, since the agency has yet to outline regulations on acceptable costs for surrogacy arrangements some couples seeking children "are dishing out more than expenses" to their surrogates. Concern about the potential for the exploitation of women in commercial surrogacy contracts was one of the major reasons for the creation of the AHRA. The fact that questionable arrangements persist three years after the passing of the legislation highlights the extent to which the role of human genetic and reproductive technologies within Canadian society remain unresolved.

Given this state of affairs, it is important to keep pushing the debate about the AHRA and its potential effectiveness beyond the realm of politics with a capital "P" and into the broader context in which the legislation will ultimately operate. In other words, it is crucial to keep questions related to women's bodies and to global capitalism in play if we are to avoid losing sight of the social and economic forest for the regulatory trees.

The fertility industry continues to grow, apparently unfettered, in the face of inaction and political conflict.

The Terms of the Act

For those concerned about the social implications of HGRTs, the act is, relative to legislation passed elsewhere in the world, a fairly progressive piece of legislation. The U.S.-based Center for Genetics and Society claims that this is at least in part because its authors arrived at their determinations by drawing on the input of a broad range of constituencies, including members of the women's health community. According to its supporters, the legislation is welcome because it draws clear boundaries "prohibiting unacceptable applications of the new technologies while allowing beneficial applications in a socially accountable manner" (Center for Genetics and Society, 2004). It does so by banning those practices that have caused most concern among feminists and others on the left—the exploitation of poor women through commercial surrogacy, sex selection (except to prevent, diagnose, or treat a sex-linked disorder), and cloning—and by permitting but regulating procedures such as sperm and egg donation, which are now viewed by many in these camps as central components of reproductive freedom. Other prohibited practices include the development of human embryos solely for research; the alteration of human DNA that would pass from one generation to the next; the creation of human/nonhuman hybrids and chimeras; and the sale of sperm, eggs, embryos, or any other human reproductive material. Research involving human embryos, including stem cell research, is permitted using embryos created but not used during in vitro fertilization and abortion procedures. The act also allows for the continuation of non-commercial surrogate mothering alongside the donation of sperm, eggs, and other reproductive material.

The Public Response

Certain sections of the new law are still contested (Center for Genetics and Society, 2004). Some organizations representing fertility clinics and infertile couples objected to the ban on payments for sperm and women's eggs citing an already precarious supply of reproductive materials in Canada (Mulholland, 2004). Antichoice groups were unhappy with the legislation for allowing any form of embryonic research and for leaving the meaning of "human being" undefined (Campaign Life Coalition, 2004). On the other end of the political spectrum, disability rights activists have called for tighter restrictions on preimplantation genetic testing to avoid promoting a medical model of disability. As Catherine Frazee noted in a 2002 speech to the ARCH Disability Law Centre:

> The bill prohibits identifying the sex of an embryo created for reproductive purposes. However, and perhaps not surprisingly, it places no comparable restriction upon the identification of disability-related characteristics. If sex selection symbolically declares females of less worth than males, then isn't it equally true that disability selection symbolically declares people with disabilities of less worth than nondisabled people? (Frazee, 2002)

Other detractors included representatives of the genetic and reproductive technology industries, alongside critics on the left, who, for different reasons, argued that the criminal sanctions for prohibited activities are excessive (Valverde & Weir, 1997). For those of us concerned about intensified criminalization and the growth of the prison-industrial complex in Canada, these certainly represent valid concerns.

Moreover, as Mariana Valverde and Lorna Weir (1997) have argued, while some feminist concerns were addressed by the report of the Royal Commission (around commercial surrogacy, for instance), questions pertaining to democratic control over commercial genetic research, and the incorporation of Aboriginal women's disquiet about Eurocentric and individualistic notions of health and family, were largely overlooked.

Disability rights activists have called for tighter restrictions on preimplantation genetic testing to avoid promoting a medical model of disability.

The provision to permit legislative review after three years, however, allowed those who were not completely happy with the measure, but thought that it was better than nothing, to support it. Witnesses at Senate hearings argued that it was particularly important to pass the act in order to end what the *Vancouver Sun* called "Canada's dubious distinction as the only Western country without a regulatory framework on embryonic technologies" (Greenaway, 2004, p. A5).

Women's Bodies and the Stem Cell Debate

The act constructs embryos and their medical use, in Rebecca Sullivan's (2005) words, "as part of the public good of Canada that must be protected from private sector commodification" (p. 51) in several ways: by insisting that all research be treated as public regardless of how it is funded, by prohibiting the cloning of embryos solely for the purpose of stem cell research, and by banning commercial surrogacy.

Even so, Sullivan continues, some sections of the act "create the conditions for the economic exchange of embryos as patentable therapeutics" (p. 51). Notable here are those sections that allow researchers, with the donor's written consent, to use embryos that are left over from fertility treatments and abortion clinics. Scientists only have to argue that their research is "necessary" and that there is no other way to approach a particular research question. As Abby Lippman, a McGill researcher and co-chair of the Canadian Women's Health Network points out, this leaves the door open for cloning in stem cell research since it is hard to imagine a scenario in which an interested scientist could not describe their work as "necessary." Lippman's observation thus brings into question the meaningfulness of this particular aspect of the legislation (2002, p. 2).

In her very provocative discursive analysis of the debate over the AHRA, Sullivan also suggests that by allowing embryos to be culled from regulated clinics, the act distinguishes between two kinds of embryos: "reproductive embryos," which qualify as almost human life and cannot therefore be bought and sold, and "replicative embryos," whose potentiality is not in producing life but in producing health benefits and which may therefore be inserted into a system of economic exchange. This fuzzy distinction, Sullivan argues, can be sustained because what is at stake in the AHRA is not "life" so much as "health," which is, of course, central to hegemonic national identity in Canada. Lawmakers deemed it in the best interests of the Canadian public that "surplus" embryos be used in the development of new treatments for disease and, by defining infertility as a public health issue, were also able to justify strict governmental regulation of the fertility industry.

This distinction also helps protect the most lucrative aspect of in vitro fertilization procedures—the development of patents derived from human DNA and genetic tests. We are all familiar with the images of youthful seniors glowing with health, sick children, and disabled adults, that are circulated by biotech companies and their allies in medical research and the large health foundations in order to promote the need for embryonic stem cell research. But critics like Abby Lippman argue that there is no scientific or moral imperative to do such research at this time: The reason researchers wish to clone human embryos is to mine them for stem cells, since mass production of such material would be more profitable for pharmaceutical companies (Felesky, 2002). Moreover, most illness and disability is not genetically endowed and Lippman, like others who are skeptical of the capacity of a government agency to make decisions about research "needs," argues that resources might best be directed towards adult stem cell research, which is at present under researched (Lippman, 2002).

It is beyond the confines of this commentary to make a well-developed argument for or against embryonic stem cell research. But since this issue is so closely tied to the politics of assisted human reproduction, it might be useful to reframe the dominant terms of the debate, as it has been constructed in Canada and the United States, through an analytical lens that foregrounds women's reproductive health. In popular discourse, the debate pits proponents of scientific research, who argue that such work will produce cures for a range of diseases and conditions, against pro-lifers, who are invested in the legal protection of embryos and fetuses. Left out of this picture, with its obsessive focus on the embryo as an independent entity, or on miraculous cures, is a concern with the intrusions on and the exploitation of women's bodies. Rarely mentioned, for example, is the fact that researchers hoping to secure patents on genetic tests and human genes or to clone human embryos from stem cells require women to sign away their rights to their fertilized eggs after they have, in Abby Lippman's words, "achieved a pregnancy, stopped trying, or simply run out of money" (Felesky, 2002, p. 34).

Moreover, as feminist writer Judith Levine (2002) argues, when questions about women are raised, often by pro-choice advocates, they too frequently fall into dualistic thinking due to a fear that any perceived concern about embryos will cede

"The genetic engineers gave him that birthmark as part of a sponsorship deal."

"The genetic engineers gave him that birthmark as part of a sponsorship deal," cartoon by Richard Jolly, www.CartoonStock.com. Copyright © Richard Jolly. Reproduction rights obtainable from www.CartoonStock.com.

territory to anti-choice forces. But, as Marcy Darnovsky of the Center for Genetics and Society puts it, "Ending an unwanted pregnancy is apples, and mucking around with genes is oranges" (Levine, 2002, p. 28). Pro-choice opponents of genetic modification, of creating embryos solely for the purposes of research, or of embryonic stem cell research itself, do not propose to give cells rights. Rather, they worry that cloned embryos might be used to take advantage of infertile women, that a focus on "choice" and "personal freedom" for women can lead us to overlook the potential for economic exploitation and oppression bound up with procedures such as genetic modification and stem cell research, and that human life and its various processes are becoming mere research tools or manufactured commodities.

In fact, as Rebecca Sullivan points out, while the bracketing of the abortion question in the AHRA might be read as a deliberate strategy to avoid debilitating debates about the sanctity of life at human conception, it also serves to further narrow the definition of reproductive technologies as related only to fertility assistance, rather than regulation through conception and abortion. This is significant because although women have the right to terminate a pregnancy in Canada, there is no law to say that these services must be provided or that they must be provided for free—a situation that often leaves women in more isolated or conservative parts of the country unable to find someone to do the procedure. As Sullivan writes, "By emphasizing the creation of new life for infertile people and ignoring the other side of the technologies, the government can also integrate therapeutic biotechnologies that use embryos as raw material by subsuming life under the rubric of public health and public good" (p. 52).

The Trouble with "Choice"

While the AHRA in fact does much to limit the kinds of choices available to infertile couples that have most troubled feminist critics over the past two decades—most notably commercial surrogacy—it does not, and cannot, forestall the ways the fertility industry has hijacked the language of "choice" in order to sell their products during this same period. Certainly, in terms of being able to have children, reproductive technologies offer one kind of choice to women who can afford them. But IVF clinics and biotech researchers who oppose regulation argue that public oversight impinges on women's choice in general. Of course, for some women and men, the new regulations in Canada will limit the range of alternatives their money can buy. What these regulations do not do, however, is either address the broad cultural preoccupation with the production of "perfect" babies, or the social conditions that are implicated in much infertility.

With regards to the former, it is important to note that there are two major markets for human reproductive technologies: women who wish to circumvent infertility or the need for a male partner, and couples at risk of passing on a particular genetic disorder. When the latter group opts for in vitro fertilization, they do it so that their embryos can be tested and only those that seem healthy are implanted. But the thinking behind this procedure also informs much more routinized aspects of planning and undergoing a contemporary pregnancy. Prenatal technologies such as amniocentesis and genetic screening, for example, encourage people to seek out the perfect baby, the quality child. As this occurs, more and more conditions that would be otherwise viewed as a routine part of human variation become medicalized and problematized. It is true, of course, as disability scholars and activists argue, that it can be quite challenging to look after a child with a disability or with health problems, but this difficulty has less to do with the child, than with the way society is organized. My critique here is not so much of the law itself—the answer to this preoccupation is not, I think, to ban prenatal testing or genetic screening. Rather, we must build a broader social awareness of the ways these technologies are enforcing discrimination and of the need for social structures that allow children with disabilities and their parents to have a full life.

The eugenicist tendencies enshrined in the new reproductive technologies are exacerbated by the fact that although there are still relatively low-cost, low-tech ways to help lesbians and single straight women conceive, many of the more advanced technologies are only open to the most privileged women. At the same time, we live in a culture in which poor women continue to be more frequently offered long-acting contraceptives and are discouraged from having children at all. In regard to the issue of addressing infertility "upstream" there is also a need—not recognized by the law—to address antiquated career structures that do not accommodate women, environmental degradation which effects both men and women's reproductive capacities, and the prevalence of undiagnosed STDs.

There are two major markets for human reproductive technologies: women who wish to circumvent infertility or the need for a male partner, and couples at risk of passing on a particular genetic disorder.

Cloning and the Global Marketplace

If truth be told, within the context of the growth of a formidable transnational biotech industry, the Canadian ban on certain terms of cloning represents a mere drop in the ocean. Jeremy Rifkin, a prominent critic of the industry, revealed in a 2001 column for the *Los Angeles Times* that in January 2000, the British patent office granted a patent to Dr. Ian Wilmut—creator of Dolly the sheep—for his cloning technology. The patent, now owned by the Geron Corporation, covers the cloning process and all the animals that are produced by it. What is not widely known, however, is that the Geron patent also covers all cloned human embryos up to the blastocyst stage of development (the stage where stem cells emerge). By allowing companies like Geron to claim embryos as intellectual property between conception and birth, do we, Rifkin asks, "risk a new era where the creation of life itself will fall under the control of commercial forces?" And he adds that "failure to examine the commercial implications of embryo and stem cell research could trap us in a commercial eugenics future that we neither anticipated nor chose."

Even as the AHRA has been ratified and the new regulatory body established, the march towards such a future continues apace. Biotechnologies in Canada are, for Rebecca Sullivan, "ushering in a postmodern society of fragmented identities not merely at the level of the social, but also at the level of our genetic material, which is increasingly being viewed as a natural resource that will lead us to greater prosperity and well-being as a nation" (p. 41). This is evidenced by, among other things, the Canadian government's substantial investment in genetic research through Genome Canada ($600 million by February 2006) and its aim to see Canada emerge as one of the top five industrial leaders in the biotechnological sector by 2010 (www.genomecanada.ca; Sullivan, 2005). Indeed, according to the Canadian Biotechnology Advisory Committee, Canada already ranks second in number of biotech firms and third in revenue generation among all nations (Sullivan, 2005).

The question that emerges from all of this, it seems to me, is: How might we prevent the emergence of what Rifkin calls a "commercial eugenics civilization" in the name of public health and social equality, while also supporting women's ability to control their fertility? Moreover, how might we do this within a framework that is cognizant of the fact that Canadian legislation is not impermeable to transnational capitalism and other agents of geneticization within and outside of the nation-state?

Acknowledgements

I wish to thank Radhika V. Mongia and Kim Sawchuk for their extremely helpful comments on an earlier version of this article.

References

Brennan, Richard. (2007) Fertility panel panned. *Globe & Mail*, p. A7.

Campaign Life Coalition. (2004). *Senate vote will open the floodgates.* News release, March 14. URL: http://www.campaignlifecoalition.com/press/2004/040314senatevote.html.

Center for Genetics and Society. (2004). *Canadian parliament approves the 'Assisted Human Reproduction Act,' a model of responsible policy.* URL: http://www.genetics-and -society.org/policies/other/canada.html.

Felesky, Leigh. (2002). Conceivable options: The future of procreation. An Interview with Abby Lippman [Bill C-56]. *Herizons*, 16(2): 34.

Frazee, Catherine. (2002). *Truth and consequences: Disability in a genetic era.* Remarks made at the ARCH Disability Law Centre General Meeting. URL: http://www.arch disabilitylaw.ca/publications/archAlert/2002/03_aug01/ 03_agm.asp.

Gazze, Mary. (2007, June 26). Canada: Destination for Infertile Couples. *Globe & Mail*, p A12.

Greenaway, Norma. (2004, March 4). Canada close to enacting stem-cell, cloning law. *Vancouver Sun*, p. A5.

Levine, Judith. (2002). What human genetic modification means for women. *World Watch*, July/August: 26-29.

Lippman, Abby. (2002). Canada's Bill C-56: Half full or half empty. *GeneWatch*, 15(5). URL: http://www.gene -watch.org/genewatch/articles/15-5c56.html.

Lippman, Abby & Nisker, Jeff.(2006). June 2006: Health Canada delay endangers women. *Canadian Centre for Policy Alternatives.* URL: http://www.policyalternatives.ca/Monitor Issues/2006/06/MonitorIssue/1390/index.cfm?pa=ddc3f905.

Mulholland, Angela. (2004, March 4). Infertile couples disappointed with cloning bill. *CTV.ca.* URL: http://www.ctv .ca/servlet/ArticleNews/print/CTVNews/20040304/cloning _bill_feature_04.

Rifkin, Jeremy. (2001, July 23). Will companies hold control of life made in a petri dish. *Los Angeles Times*, p. B11.

Sullivan, Rebecca. (2005). An embryonic nation: Life against health in Canadian biotechnological discourse. *Communication Theory*, 15(1): 39-58.

Valverde, Marianne. & Weir, Lorna. (1997). Regulating new reproductive and genetic technologies: A feminist view of recent Canadian government initiatives. *Feminist Studies*, 23(2): 418-423.

In Ireland, Human Embryos Should Be Treated as Human Life

Kevin Doran

Father Kevin Doran is a Catholic priest and the secretary general of the 2012 International Eucharistic Congress in Dublin, Ireland. In the following viewpoint, he argues that the Irish Council for Bioethics has left the door open for cloning and manipulating human embryos. The council should declare embryos to be persons, he insists, and should reject such genetic manipulation.

As you read, consider the following questions:

1. What does Doran say is the relationship between personhood and personality?

2. According to the Irish Council for Bioethics (ICB), what is the difference between reproductive cloning and therapeutic cloning?

3. Why does Doran believe that there was no clear answer in the ICB report as to whom should fund embryonic stem cell research?

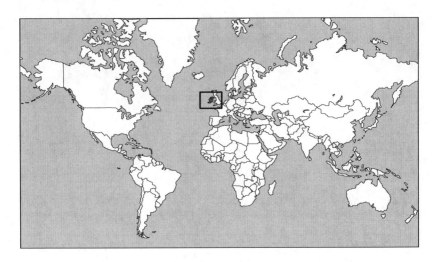

The idea of the Irish Council for Bioethics [(ICB) an independent body established by the Irish government] granting "significant moral value" to human embryos would be amusing, if it were not so arrogant.

Self-Evident Rights

Last week's [in April 2008] opinion published by the council said: "On consideration of the various arguments relating to the moral status of the embryo, the council adopts a gradualist position, granting significant moral value, rather than full moral status, to human embryos. The moral value they are seen to possess is based on recognition of their potential to develop into persons, as well as the value they derive from representing human life in its earliest stages."

In initial discussions 18 months ago, I indicated that Catholics had some difficulty with the idea of "assigning rights" to the embryo, which was the terminology the council was proposing at the time. My problem is that this might be taken to imply a reference to civil or discretionary rights. The Catholic perspective is that the rights of the embryo derive from its nature and, in that sense, are human rights, the kind that would be described in some documents as self-evident. Such rights are not assigned or granted (as the report now suggests).

The obligation to respect life begins at the point when individual human life begins—or even when there is a reasonable possibility that it may have begun. The council rejects the argument that the embryo is a person, on the grounds that personhood implies characteristic personal activity (or sentience). But human or personal activity is the *result* of being a person, not the cause of it. The council seems to be falling into the common trap of confusing "person" and "personality." The embryo is a person, but it doesn't have personality.

The opinion said that the council believes that "the moral value of human embryos that will otherwise remain frozen or be destroyed needs to be balanced against the moral value of human welfare, which is likely to increase with advances in medical science that ameliorate quality of life. While accepting the value of human life demands that we hold significant respect for embryos, it also demands that we consider our obligations to care for humankind more generally. The council would, therefore, consider embryonic stem cell research to be acceptable in certain contexts."

The obligation to respect life begins at the point when individual human life begins—or even when there is a reasonable possibility that it may have begun.

While the council said it did not think that the creation of embryos specifically for research was currently justified or represented a proportional response while "supernumerary IVF embryos" [that is, embryos left over from in vitro fertilization (IVF) efforts] existed, it reserved the right to re-evalute the balance between ethical concerns and the value to society of such research if IVF processes become more efficient, with a resulting drop in the number of "supernumerary embryos"

available for research, or if the therapeutic potential of somatic cell nuclear transfer (SCNT) was borne out by research.

Utilitarian Ethics

The underlying ethos of the council's opinion is predomi-
nantly utilitarian. In effect it says: "We would prefer not to destroy embryos, but if it seems to serve a useful purpose, we
will." It is easier, of course, to make this kind of judgment if
one sees oneself as *granting* moral value to the embryo.

Similarly, the opinion that embryos should not be generated specifically for research, is subject to a utilitarian caveat.
The council effectively says: "If supplies of embryos from IVF
dry up, then we might reconsider this." In other words, the
council has no principled objection.

But then the bioethics council goes on to argue against the
undue instrumentalisation of human life. Is there a principle
anywhere in all of this?

It is good that the council recognises cloned embryos as
having the same value as so-called "supernumerary embryos".
Unfortunately, this is a rather limited value.

There are a number of important issues around the use of
terminology.

---

*Any distinction between "therapeutic" and "reproductive"
cloning is unscientific and spurious, and appears
designed to facilitate the use of embryos for research.*

The report said the council "supports the carefully regulated use of supernumerary IVF embryos—that are otherwise
destined to be destroyed—for the purposes of embryonic stem
cell research aimed at alleviating human suffering. The decision to donate supernumerary embryos for research should be
voluntary, free from any form of coercion and made under
the strict conditions of informed consent". The designation of
certain embryos as "surplus" or "supernumerary" tends to im-

ply that they are of less value, or that they are less entitled to be protected. It suggests that, by using them for research, they are given some value, whereas otherwise they would die uselessly. This view also flows from the underlying utilitarian ethos of the opinion. Objectively speaking, the value of so-called "supernumerary embryos" is exactly the same as that of any other embryo. They are only "destined" to die because of the decisions that people have made about them.

In the opinion, a distinction is made between "reproductive cloning", for the purposes of transmitting life to a new human being, and "therapeutic cloning", which would be for the purpose of obtaining embryos for biomedical research. In reality, whatever its ultimate purpose and whatever terminology people may choose to employ, human cloning is *always* reproductive, in that the immediate result of cloning is the generation of a human being. It is never "therapeutic", in the generally understood sense of the term, because it never contributes to the health or well-being of the embryo who is the subject of research. Any distinction between "therapeutic" and "reproductive" cloning is unscientific and spurious, and appears designed to facilitate the use of embryos for research.

Animal-Human Embryos

On the topic of animal-human chimeras, the report said: "If the creation of embryos for research were deemed to be acceptable at some point in the future, the council would have no principled objection to the creation of human-animal hybrid cell lines, which would obviate concerns relating to coercion and exploitation of women".

An embryo may be cloned using an animal ovum (egg), where the animal nucleus is removed and replaced with the nucleus of a human cell. As the ICB notes in the document, this does not mean that all of the animal DNA has been removed. Some small—but potentially significant—amount of animal DNA is left in the mitochondria of the cell, and even-

The Catholic Church on Genetic Engineering

Some have imagined the possibility of using techniques of genetic engineering to introduce alterations with the presumed aim of improving and strengthening the gene pool. Some of these proposals exhibit a certain dissatisfaction or even rejection of the value of the human being as a finite creature and person. Apart from technical difficulties and the real and potential risks involved, such manipulation would promote a eugenic [attempting to improve or perfect human genetic makeup] mentality and would lead to indirect social stigma with regard to people who lack certain qualities, while privileging qualities that happen to be appreciated by a certain culture or society; such qualities do not constitute what is specifically human. This would be in contrast with the fundamental truth of the equality of all human beings which is expressed in the principle of justice, the violation of which, in the long run, would harm peaceful coexistence among individuals. Furthermore, one wonders who would be able to establish which modifications were to be held as positive and which not, or what limits should be placed on individual requests for improvement since it would be materially impossible to fulfill the wishes of every single person. . . . All of this leads to the conclusion that the prospect of such an intervention would end sooner or later by harming the common good, by favouring the will of some over the freedom of others. Finally it must also be noted that in the attempt to create *a new type of human being* one can recognize *an ideological element* in which man tries to take the place of his Creator.

Congregation for the Doctrine of the Faith,
"Instruction Dignitas Personae on Certain Bioethical Questions,"
Vatican, June 20, 2008.

tually becomes part of the new organism. It is not clear what this DNA will do, or how it will affect the development of the embryo. The ICB seems to justify this on the basis that the embryo will not, in any case, be allowed to develop. But once again the council dodges the question as to what exactly this embryo is.

Crucially, the opinion of the Irish Council for Bioethics does not reflect the outcome of its public consultation. According to the council's own analysis of the consultation, respondents were fairly well balanced between men and women and there were more respondents under 45 than over.

A huge majority of these were opposed to research using embryonic stem cells, the generation of embryos specifically for research or the generation of hybrid human-animal embryos.

Crucially, the opinion of the Irish Council for Bioethics does not reflect the outcome of its public consultation.

There are risks in determining ethics by public consultation, because popular opinion doesn't always reflect the truth. But it does seem odd that the opinion of the council is so much at variance with the public perception of this issue.

The one question to which there seemed to be no very clear answer was who should fund embryonic stem cell research, if it were allowed in Ireland. Presumably this is because the vast majority of those who might be expected to meet these costs believe such research shouldn't be permitted.

In Japan, Some Genetic Manipulation of Human Embryos Is Acceptable

Satoshi Kodama and Akira Akabayashi

Satoshi Kodama is an assistant professor and Akira Akabayashi is a professor of biomedical ethics at the Graduate School of Medicine at the University of Tokyo. In the following viewpoint, they discuss Japanese efforts to decide on an ethical approach to the treatment of human embryos in cloning and harvesting of stem cells. The authors say that Japanese ethics committees did not use Western ethical categories but instead defined the embryo as the "sprout of life." Thus, embryos had some ethical standing but were not considered fully human life. As a result, the authors say, Japan allowed for some regulated experimentation on human embryos.

As you read, consider the following questions:

1. What was the first point debated by the cloning sub-committee with respect to regulations on human cloning, according to the authors?

2. According to Professor Saku Machino, how does human genetic engineering violate article 13 of the Japanese constitution?

Satoshi Kodama and Akira Akabayashi, *Contested Cells: Global Perspectives on the Stem Cell Debate*, London: Imperial College Press. 2010, pp. 422, 425–434. Copyright © 2010 by The Imperial College Press. All rights reserved. Reproduced by permission.

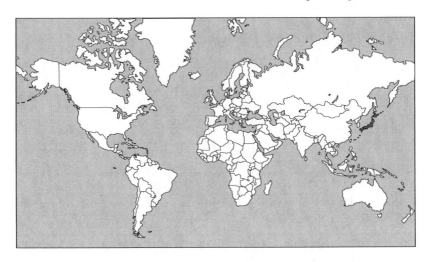

3. What Western terms and discussion do the authors say
   is close to the Japanese term "sprout of life"?

The birth of Dolly, the cloned sheep, was reported worldwide in February 1997. The communiqué issued by the
Denver summit of the G8 [Group of Eight, a forum made up
of the governments of eight major economies] held in June of
the same year acknowledged concerns about the creation of
cloned humans, and noted the necessity of both domestic and
international efforts to regulate cloning. In September, the
Bioethics Committee was established as a division of the
Council for Science and Technology within the former Japanese Prime Minister's office. . . .

The Cloning Subcommittee
Discussions Regarding the Regulation
of Human Cloning

The two main points that were debated with respect to regulations on human cloning were: (1) whether 'human dignity'
could be used as the basis for such regulations and (2) whether
regulations should be in the form of laws or administrative
guidelines.

The main points of the discussions regarding the regulation of human cloning that took place within the cloning subcommittee are summarised as follows. First, the committee discussed the issue of human cloning separately from the issue of animal cloning. They considered animal cloning to be highly useful and beneficial, and determined that regulation was not urgently needed. In the case of human cloning, on the other hand, although there are individuals with identical genetic characteristics (i.e., identical twins), the subcommittee concluded that the intentional creation of clones for *reproductive purposes* violates human dignity. The subcommittee's reasoning was that nuclear transplantation cloning [where genetic material from one individual to be cloned is injected into another individual's egg] is a form of asexual reproduction, and thus lacks the element of 'chance at the genetic level' that accompanies normal sexual reproduction. The subcommittee also concluded that the production of cloned organs for transplants should be prohibited, because this also involves the creation of human clones (implanting cloned embryos in the uterus). However, the subcommittee decided that cloning for the purposes of investigating cellular structure should be permitted, because such research is of great value, and, lacking any reproductive ends, does not violate human dignity.

The draft of the report produced by the cloning subcommittee ... concluded the following regarding the regulation of human cloning:

> The production of human clones, due to what accompanies this production, could lead to the breeding of humans, could turn humans into a means to an end, and/or into tools. This can also result in a deviation from the ways of thinking about reproduction, i.e., asexual reproduction. This will bring about disruption of the family order and cause problems related to the safety of those born. Furthermore, the serious issue unique to human cloning is the intentional production of people with duplicate genetic characteristics.

This may lead to the violation of the resulting cloned child's human rights, and clearly violates the constitutional principle of respect for individuals. Therefore, the intentional production of cloned human individuals should be completely prohibited due to the magnitude of the negative effects, and it would be appropriate to regulate cloning using the binding force of law.

On the other hand, the committee concluded that research that did not involve the creation of individual clones should be regulated using administrative guidelines and not prohibited by law, because it was very likely that such research would prove to be highly useful in the future.

The subcommittee concluded that the intentional creation of clones for reproductive purposes *violates human dignity.*

Human Dignity

Upon receiving the report from the cloning subcommittee, the Bioethics Committee's discussion focused primarily on the meaning of 'dignity' and the significance of making distinctions between human beings and animals.

First, there were questions about whether 'dignity' could serve as the legal basis for regulation. In particular, as the following comment demonstrates, the issue was whether or not the German principle of 'human dignity' can be derived from the Japanese constitution.

The very question of whether the German principle of "human dignity" exists in the Japanese constitution has been controversial, although the constitution does contain the principle of respect for the individual. I think it is a bit difficult to go straight from the idea of human dignity to specific legal regulation. On the other hand, I think it would be easier to set up legal regulations based on the idea of harm

179

to others, or disruption of public order, although there are also strong counterarguments against that as well.

Related to this first problem, a second issue emerged when it was pointed out that a clear rationale should be given for permitting the creation of animal clones while forbidding those of human. The next comment, for example, was typical:

> The report says it is wrong to produce offspring without the involvement of both sexes, and to intentionally produce individuals that are genetically identical. In fact, we are already doing this with animals. By this logic, we are violating the dignity of animals, so I think we need to clearly explain why it is wrong only in the case of humans.

Other comments also demonstrate scepticism toward drawing a well-defined line between humans and animals, and as the following quote shows, some argued that this way of thinking was Western rather than Asian:

> There can be no doubt that the idea that humans possess a special mission different from animals is emphasised within the Christian tradition. I think it is also true that it was on this basis that the modern concept of human dignity was established. So I think it's natural that this idea should seem out of place when considered from an Asian, or Japanese, perspective.

Through these discussions, the Bioethics Committee came to define human cloning as both a violation of human dignity, and a violation of human rights (*vis-à-vis* the children born through cloning). The connection between human dignity and human rights was pointed out by Kyoto University law professor Ryuichi Ida (a specialist in constitutional and international law), who was a member of both the cloning subcommittee and the human embryo subcommittee. Professor Ida explained that human rights were at the core of the principle of human

International Cloning Laws

There is no federal law banning cloning in the United States, but several states have passed their own laws to ban the practice. The U.S. Food and Drug Administration (FDA) has also said that anyone in the United States attempting human cloning must first get its permission. In Japan, human cloning is a crime that is punishable by up to 10 years in prison. England has allowed cloning human embryos, but is working to pass legislation to stop total human cloning.

Roderick L. Fennell, The Future of Tomorrow: How Technology, Medicine, Computers, and Travel Will Change Beyond the 21st Century. *Bloomington, IN: Author House, 2007.*

dignity. Sophia University law professor Saku Machino (an expert in criminal law), echoing Professor Ida's opinion, commented as follows:

> Basically, there are two steps, I think ... first, we have human dignity, which is a very abstract value—the value of our civilisation. And then, we have a *violation* of human dignity, which takes a concrete shape when individual rights are violated, as Professor Ida ... mentioned. That's how we conceive the relationship between human dignity and human rights.

Legal Regulation or Administrative Guidelines?

Both the cloning subcommittee and the human embryo subcommittee ultimately supported legal regulation over administrative guidelines. The reasoning behind this was explained by Professor Machino. His argument can be summarised as follows:

Although administrative guidelines have an advantage in that they can be applied more flexibly than laws, they lack binding power insofar as they have no legal basis. Thus it is not possible to penalise violators through the use of sanctions. In the case of legal regulation on the other hand, those orders can be imbued with binding force. Laws enacted by the National Diet [i.e., the Japanese parliamentary assembly] also have an advantage over administrative guidelines because they are established through democratic procedures. In the case of cloning regulation in particular, it is really best if these things are debated in the Diet as it may limit constitutional rights such as freedom of scholarship or reproductive rights.

The very question of whether the German principle of "human dignity" exists in the Japanese constitution has been controversial.

On the other hand, as a general rule the fact that something is immoral does not alone justify the use of legal coercion. To justify such a step, there must be a violation of interests protected by law. But the creation of human clones violates the principle of 'respect for individuals', in the sense that 'all people must be respected as unique entities with unique personalities' because it is an activity that involves creating humans with genetic characteristics copied from people already existing. And thus it violates article 13 of the constitution, which states that, 'All people shall be respected as individuals'. The creation of chimera embryos or hybrid embryos by fusing human and animal embryos also damages the integrity of the human species, and the production of incomplete individuals is an act that violates the dignity of those produced. Therefore this could be said to violate the respect for individuals stipulated in article 13.

Nonetheless, the drawback of legal regulation is that it may have a chilling effect on research. Thus it is best to legally prohibit only the creation of human clones, and regulate research using human embryos with administrative guidelines.

Following this discussion, the Bioethics Committee ultimately released a short document . . . dated December 21, 1999. Its main points were as follows: (1) cloning by transplantation of somatic cell nuclei [which is controversial as the first step in reproductive cloning] will be prohibited, but clones made using nuclear transplantation from early embryos and the creation of multiple individuals through the division of early embryos will be regulated by means other than law, (2) creation of individual organisms using chimera or hybrid embryos [that is, with both human and animal DNA] will be prohibited, (3) guidelines will be drawn up by the human embryo subcommittee in order to regulate the production of human embryos for research purposes, and (4) these points will be reviewed in three to five years given the need for international harmony and release of information to the public.

Human Embryo Research

The draft of the report . . . released in March 6, 2000, by the Subcommittee on Human Embryo Research, states that human embryos (including cloned embryos) are the 'sprout of human life' and would require considerate, rather than frivolous, treatment. Therefore research should be permitted within an appropriate regulatory framework. The expression 'sprout of human life' (*seimei no houga*) was first used in the draft of the law on cloning technology within the cloning subcommittee that met on May 12 of the previous year. Within the subcommittee it was explained that the concept of 'sprout of life' is different from 'life' itself, and research using human embryos should be permitted in certain situations because 'the harm in violation of embryos that are no more than a sprout of life is minute relative to that of foetuses or humans'.

The subcommittee's report stated the following:

This subcommittee holds that human embryos existing outside of the uterus are the sprout of human life and require
careful handling, but they are still at a different stage than
foetuses or postnatal humans. Therefore, embryos which
have been set to be disposed of can be used in research
deemed scientifically and morally appropriate.... Particularly in light of the establishment of embryonic stem cell research, which requires a swift response in Japan and is the
source of high hopes for regenerative medicine, we judge after considerable consideration that the use of human embryos should be permitted.

---

*A human embryo is potentially a person, but it is not yet
a person. Therefore, its destruction is not the same as
murder.*

The subcommittee suggested that specific regulations on research using human embryos include the following: (1) only
frozen surplus embryos [that is, embryos that would otherwise be discarded] would be used, (2) consent from the couple
would be required, (3) no compensation would be provided
for the embryos, (4) research would be limited to basic research initially, and no clinical research would be performed,
and (5) research would require review by an ethics committee.
Furthermore, as embryonic stem cells [embryo cells that can
divide and change into other cells and that are highly valued
in research] do not result in creation of an individual human,
the committee deemed that legal regulation was not necessary
and opted for more flexible guidelines. In addition, the subcommittee proposed a moratorium on the use of cloned embryos for the following reasons: (1) it might lead to the creation of human clones, (2) the creation and subsequent
destruction of a cloned embryo for research purposes is, morally speaking, on par with doing the same thing to a human

embryo and hence undesirable, (3) stem cell research using surplus embryos, which is less problematic than use of cloned embryos, should proceed first, and (4) based on the results of research using surplus embryos, the propriety of using cloned embryos should be reexamined.

The 'Sprout of Human Life'

A fascinating exchange occurred regarding the expression 'sprout of human life', between committee member Norio Fujisawa, a prominent researcher of Greek philosophy, and legal scholar Ryuichi Ida.

Fujisawa noted:

> Consider the issue in really commonsensical terms: from the standpoint of science you can rationalise it in all sorts of ways and argue that an embryo is the sprout of life, but not life. Yet, I think that maybe to the ethical sensibility of a normal person, they might be inclined to think that the sprout of life is the same as life.

To which Ida responded as follows:

> Well, of course, if born, this becomes a "person". And legally it is possible a foetus would be treated as a person as well. However, a human embryo itself has not yet become a foetus ..., so I think it is extremely difficult to judge whether this should be thought of as being the same as a person.... Because it is at the embryo stage, a stage at which it has not yet fully developed into a foetus, isn't it rather difficult to call it human life? Having said that, an embryo is not just a "thing" either; if it divides, it will naturally become a person. This is why we used the expression "sprout of human life", and thus in a sense it describes an intermediate stage on the way to becoming a person.... In embryonic stem cell research, embryos are created, and the created embryos are destroyed. If the embryo was deemed to be human life, then to take it to an extreme, these researchers would be committing murder. The embryo protection law in Ger-

many, for instance, reflects such a position, and thus human embryo research is not possible there. But to hold the position of wanting to conduct human embryo research if possible, or even to a certain extent, you essentially draw a line to signify that it is acceptable to do certain types of research but not others. In this case, I think that a rationale—that embryos are not human life—is necessary to some degree. And that is why I say that human embryos are the sprout of human life.

In response, Fujisawa asked:

So then, in terms of ancient philosophical concepts, there's potentiality and actuality. Are you saying that embryos basically constitute the potentiality of life, but not the actuality?

Both Ida and the chair, [Hiro] Imura, responded that Fujisawa was correct. It's not clear whether the two of them fully understood Fujisawa's question, which was based on the thinking of Aristotle. However, the exchange suggests that the expression 'sprout of human life' is close to the discussion of 'potentiality', which has been the centre of contention in debates over the artificial termination of pregnancy in English-speaking countries. Thus, a human embryo is potentially a person, but it is not yet a person. Therefore, its destruction is not the same as murder.

In the end, this report was accepted by the Bioethics Committee, and the committee's views were compiled in a final report. . . . At the same time, the regulation of human cloning techniques bill drafted by the government in accordance with the reports by the cloning subcommittee and human embryo subcommittee was presented and explained, and the committee was adjourned. The bill was submitted to the National Diet on April 14, 2000. The *Law Concerning Regulations Relating to Human Cloning Techniques and Other Similar Techniques* was passed on November 30, 2000, and went into effect on June 6, 2001.

Islamic Scholars Oppose Human Cloning Based on Social Practice and Ethics

Abdulaziz Sachedina

Abdulaziz Sachedina, an American citizen born in Tanzania, is a professor of religious studies at the University of Virginia, Charlottesville. In the following viewpoint, he says that Islamic scholars see cloning as disrupting family structures and lineages. He says that, on those grounds, they see cloning for therapeutic purposes as being acceptable in some situations. However, he says that Muslim scholars have argued that even research on therapeutic cloning at this time would be immoral, because of the high cost of such research and the need to direct resources to more pressing problems, including poverty and common disease eradication.

As you read, consider the following questions:

1. According to Sachedina, what is the precautionary principle in Shari'a law?
2. Why does Sachedina say that Muslims regard international law with mistrust?

Abdulaziz Sachedina, "The Cultural and the Religious in Islamic Biomedicine: The Case of Human Cloning," *Cross-Cultural Issues in Bioethics: The Example of Human Cloning*, edited by in Heiner Roetz, New York, NY: Rodopi B.V. Amsterdam, 2006, pp. 268–272, 284–285. Copyright © 2006 by Rodopi B.V. Amsterdam. All rights reserved. Reproduced by permission.

3. Why may Muslim scholars not consider cloning to be exactly "creation," according to Sachedina?

Since the cloning of Dolly, the sheep, in 1997 a number of Muslim scholars have, on the one hand, deliberated on the ethics of human cloning and, on the other, on the relationship between religion and science, and religion and culture. The urgency and even crisis situation created by the cloning debate in the Muslim world has led to an unprecedented interfaith cooperation in formulating a proper response to the possibility of human cloning and the adverse ways in which this scientific advancement will affect human society in general, and human relationships in particular. Majority of the Muslim legists' [legal experts'] ethical-legal rulings studied for this [viewpoint] show that these concerns are centered on the cloned person's hereditary relationship to the owner of the cell and the egg, and the relational ramifications of that to the other individuals in the child's immediate families. It is not difficult to see that religious-ethical questions are spurred by cultural sensitivities regarding an individual's identity within familial and extended social relationships. In addition, there are questions about the ways human cloning will affect the culture of intense concern with a person's religious and social distinctiveness. It is precisely at this juncture that cross-cultural communication between Muslim and Christian scholars assumes a front position in highlighting cultural variations among their communities. Whereas individuality of a cloned human being is central to much discussion in the Western-Christian cultures, it is the concern with a child's lineage, familial and social relationships that dominates the Muslim cultural sensitivities.

One of the most important studies dealing with the subject in Arabic is: *al-Istinsakh bayna al-islam wa al-masihiyva* (Cloning in Islam and Christianity). The study aims to demonstrate plurality as well as mutuality among the cultures of the people in the Middle East. Leading Christian, Sunni and

Shiite [two major Muslim denominations] scholars, representing shared cultural concerns while holding pluralistic opinions in their respective traditions, have contributed to the debate on the way in which human cloning will adversely impact upon the future of the institution of marriage and parent-child relations. The interfaith discourse is based on a common concern in these communities, namely, concern with the negative impact of human cloning on the culture of human interaction.

Whereas individuality of a cloned human being is central to much discussion in the Western-Christian cultures, it is the concern with a child's lineage, familial and social relationships that dominate the Muslim cultural sensitivities.

To be sure, the guiding principle regarding any scientific advancement in Islam is the cautious note in the sacred law of Islam, the Shari'a. The precautionary note in the Shari'a takes into consideration the norm that there is seldom a thing of benefit without some inherent disadvantage affecting people's religion, life, lineage, reason and property. Islam's concern to combine noble ends with noble means rules out the idea of good end justifying a corrupt means. Taking the specific case of human cloning, the most important rule is avoidance of anything that might adversely affect human nature and human relationships. Islam forbids any tampering with human nature in any way other than legitimate methods of correction. Anything that is done for prevention or as treatment is legitimate. Ethical judgment on medical procedure is made on the basis of predominance of benefit (*istislah*) that requires rejection of probable harm (*daf' al-darar al-muhtamal*).

The Will of God

Following the euphoria over the latest success in animal cloning in 1997 prominent Muslim scholars representing both

Sunni and Shiite centers of religious learning in the Middle East . . . , expressed their opinions on human cloning. Some of these opinions are regarded as official Sunni and Shiite positions. The Arabic term used for this process in the legal as well as journalistic literature is indicative of the widespread speculation and popular perception regarding the goal of this technology, namely, *istinsakh,* meaning 'clone, copy of the original.' This interpretive meaning is not very different from the fictional cloning portrayed in *In His Image: The Cloning of a Man* by David Rorvik in the 1970s when cloning by nuclear transplantation [when genetic material to be cloned is placed into an unfertilized egg] was the topic of the day in North America. It is also because of the popular misperception about human "copies that can be produced at will through cloning" that the leading mufti of Egypt, Dr. Nasr Farid Wasil in Cairo, declared human cloning as a satanic act of disbelief and corruption that would change the nature with which God created human beings, thereby impacting negatively upon social order and practice. Accordingly, his juridical decision was that the technology had to be regulated and controlled by the government to protect Muslim society from such an inevitable harm.

However, this position was disputed by another leading Egyptian legist Yusuf al-Qaradawi who, when asked if cloning was interference in the creation of God or an affront to God's will, asserted in no unclear terms:

> Oh no, no one can challenge or oppose God's will. Hence, if the matter is accomplished then it is certainly under the will of God. Nothing can be created without God's will facilitating its creation. As long as humans continue to do so, it is the will of God. Actually, we do not raise the question whether it is in accord with the will of God. Our question is whether the matter is licit or not.

Although in these early rulings the issue of cloning technology was not given much serious consideration in Muslim ethical-religious discussions of cellular nuclear transplantation, . . .

there is much concern with anticipated biological and social effects of cloning on the underlying Islamic ethical framework and social fabric as discussed by al-Qaradawi. In brief, al-Qaradawi raises a fundamental question about the impact of this technology on the human life:

> Would such a process create disorder in human life when human beings with their subjective opinions and caprices interfere in God's created nature on which He has created people and has founded their life on it? It is only then that we can assess the gravity of the situation created by the possibility of cloning a human being, that is, to copy numerous faces of a person as if they were carbon copies of each other.

Cloning and Family

The fundamental ethical question based on the laws of nature, as al-Qaradawi states, centers around a consideration whether this procedure interferes with growing up in a family that is founded upon fatherhood and motherhood. It is in a family that the child is nurtured to become a person. In addition, al-Qaradawi says, since God has placed in each man and woman an instinct to procreate this individual in the family, why would there be a need of marriage if an individual could be created by cloning? Such a procedure may even lead to a male not in need of a female companion, except for carrying the embryo to full gestation. Moreover, such an imbalance in the nature will lead to the corruption of human society, "leading to the illicit relationship between man and man and woman and woman, as it has happened in some Western countries." This reference to "Western" culture needs to be understood as the central issue in our search for cross-cultural communication about Islamic values of family life that would be affected by an invasive biotechnology.

In general, Muslim religious attitude has regarded Western European culture hegemonic in its imposition over the non-Western world. Traditional scholars have resisted this dominance in all areas of the modern culture in Muslim societies. The negative evaluation has been felt even in the area of international law, which is regarded by many as the product of European cultural consensus without regard to the multicultural reality of the international community. Consequently, major moral problems confronting the world today are seen as the by-product of Western materialist and antireligious culture with little regard for the spiritual and moral well-being of the people.

Cultural dislocations have evidently gripped many Muslim societies today. As a consequence of imported modernization programs without local cultural legitimacy, Muslims have suffered "cultural homelessness" in their own societies since the early part of 20th century. The emerging oppositional discourse against Western encroachment on Muslim social values has symbolically led the militant Muslims to view anything and everything coming even in the form of scientific advancement as imposition of Western values on Muslim cultures. There is a fear of the further deterioration of social and familial values that are already affected by modern secular education and pervasive "CNNization" of mass media. Initial reactions to the news about cloning that were reported in the Muslim world expressed people's deep-seated fear about further erosion of family values through cloning. To be sure, science is not viewed amorally in the Muslim world. Any human action involves cognition and volition, the two processes that determine the moral course of an action. Hence, cloning of human beings was viewed with much suspicion in the beginning, and it was only gradually that more knowledgeable analyses took place in public.

The other issue taken up by al-Qaradawi against cloning is based on the Qur'anic notion about variations and cultural diversity among peoples as a sign from God who created human beings in different forms and colors, just as He created them distinct from other animals. This plurality reflects the richness of life. However, cloning might take away this diversity. A semblance through "copying" might even lead to the errors of marital relationship where spouses will not be able to recognize their partners, leading to serious social and ethical consequences. From the point of health also, as al-Qaradawi argues, one could presume that cloned persons, sharing the same DNA, will be afflicted by the same virus. However, he maintains that it is permissible to use the technology to cure certain hereditary diseases, such as infertility. . . .

Major moral problems confronting the world today are seen as the by-product of Western materialist and antireligious culture with little regard for the spiritual and moral well-being of the people.

It is interesting to note that among Muslim scholars there is almost no reference to eugenics [the effort to create a pure human race, most infamously associated with the Nazis] in any of the opinions studied for this [viewpoint]. In contrast, drawing from the modern European history, several Arab Christian scholars mention the danger of the abuse of cloning technology if used with the same intentions that eugenics was used for racial exclusion and generational improvement through extermination.

When we examine the Shiite rulings we notice that their legists have endorsed the cloning technology as being part of the possibilities that are actually created within the natural forms of conception. The leading Lebanese jurist, Sayyed Muhammad Hussein Fadl-Allah, in his judicial decision states:

There are two points that deserve mention: First, does such a scientific advancement [in the field of cloning] mean that humans are interfering in God's act or that it is deviation from the religion? We do not regard the biomedical advancement as interfering in God's work and against religious thought in its doctrinal concern. In fact we have argued earlier in relation to test-tube babies that such a birth is not far from God's law of creation. After all, the scientists have discovered this law. They know God's secret in the matter of procreation, by seeking to be guided by the laws that God has shaped for procreation. This is what we see in this new experiment with cloning, which is not proposing any new law of creation, nor is it formulating a new way of creation that would challenge God's power over creation. It has simply discovered some secrets of physiology and has cognized the dynamic of these secrets and its potentials in employing them to clone an animal or a human being.

Hence, what the scientists are doing is not exactly "creation"; cloning is simply employing all that is potentially within the natural sphere to bring about the conception. However, such interventions are not without harm to the accepted social norms regarding marriage and parenthood. . . .

Cloning and Justice

The recent opinions expressed by Muslim legists around the world confirm my assessment of the ethical issues associated with cloning, namely, that in providing religious guidance in matters connected with the future of humanity, Islamic norms have been studied in the context of the social and cultural conditions of Muslim societies. A unanimity has now emerged among Muslim scholars of different legal rights that whereas in Islamic tradition therapeutic uses of cloning and any research to further that goal will receive the endorsement of the major legal schools, the idea of human cloning has been viewed negatively and almost, to use the language of the mufti of Egypt, "satanic." A further recommendation among Muslims seems to be discouraging even the research aspects geared towards improvement of human health through the genetic manipulation. . . . In view of limited resources in the Islamic world and the expensive technology that is needed for research related to cloning, Muslim legists have asked their governments to ban research on cloning at this time.

Since technologically assisted reproduction in Islamic tradition is legitimized only within the lawful male-female relationship to help infertility, somatic cell nuclear transfer cloning from adult cells for therapeutic purposes will have to abide by the general criterion set for this technology. In the case of cloning specifically for the purposes of relieving human disease, there is no ethical impediment to stop such research, which on the scale of probable benefit outweighs possible harm, I believe that research in human cloning from adult cells in the course of reproduction treatment should be allowed with necessary regulatory clauses to restrict abuse under penalty. My opinion is based on the principle of 'averting (and not interdicting) causes of corruption has precedence over bringing about that which has benefit.'

In view of limited resources in the Islamic world and the expensive technology that is needed for research related to cloning, Muslim legists have asked their governments to ban research on cloning at this time.

In our religiously and ethically pluralistic societies where there is a search for a universal ethical language that can speak to the adherents of different religious and cultural traditions, Islamic tradition with its experience in dealing with matters central to human interpersonal relations in diverse cultural settings can become an important source for our ethical deliberations dealing with the ideals and realities of human existence. For instance, I am deeply concerned [about] the way we shy away from considering the subjective dimensions pertaining to human spiritual and moral awareness in setting our goals for research in human embryo. . . . On hearing my Christian and Jewish colleagues on human cloning I feel that there is a consensus to look into prioritization of national resources to achieve fair distribution of health care resources both nationally and internationally. From a standpoint of common moral commitment to the principle of distributive justice [that is, the socially just allocation of goods], it will be hard to justify a heavy investment in embryonic research related to animal cloning without addressing some immediate and serious problems of poverty around the globe. Moreover, the wealthy countries have a responsibility to share their material as well as scientific resources with other underprivileged nations whose immediate needs do not go beyond treating common diseases like malaria and tuberculosis.

Social Practices and Traditional Ethics Should Adjust to New Technologies Such as Human Cloning

Nestor Micheli Morales

Nestor Micheli Morales is an adjunct assistant professor of psychology at the City University of New York. In the following viewpoint, he says that advances in cloning have created much ideological opposition worldwide. He says that this opposition is based on emotion and prejudice rather than science. He says that clones will be unique individuals, just as identical twins are unique individuals. He argues that humans should learn to accept cloning, which is inevitable and will help the human race progress to a new stage of evolution.

As you read, consider the following questions:

1. What three types of harm do opponents of human cloning fear will result from clones, according to Morales?
2. How does Morales say clones will be affected by the fact that no two clones are born at exactly the same time or in exactly the same space?

3. What specific social benefits does Morales see resulting from human cloning?

Science and technology are advancing so fast that society has difficulties in keeping pace with the complexities that new developments bring. Human reproductive techniques have progressed rapidly in the past three decades [before 2009], and other new techniques such as cloning have been introduced.

Cloning and the Future

Speculations about the idea of cloning emerged in the early 1960s, and ideas of human cloning in particular were discussed in the 1970s, followed by some innovations in nuclear transfer [involving implantation of DNA to be cloned into an unfertilized egg] in the early 1980s. Human cloning represents asexual reproduction, and the critics of human cloning often assume that the result of cloning is not a unique individual. This has led to condemnations of human cloning from the politicians' side and to fear, ignorance, and "clonophobia" from the public's side.

The cloning debate has also been reinforced with ethical, religious, scientific, moral, medical, and political issues, since human cloning became a more plausible prospect in the late 1990s.

Emotional responses have dominated the debate on human cloning, and although emotions can sometimes be justified, many times they can be caused by prejudice. Gregory E. Pence [a medical ethics expert] maintains that physicians, bioethicists, and scientists have done poorly in helping to reduce the public's fears and misconceptions. For several years, research on cloning has been placed at the center of interest and debate among scientists of different disciplines. [Psychologist George] Albee, for example, argues that there is increasing political pressure on science and scientists in respect of issues such as cloning and genetic engineering, whose implications are important and gradually affect major national and political decisions.

The critics of human cloning, however, argue that there are many unaddressed problems, among them the implications of the harm issue. Other important concerns are related to family, such as family interactions (in the case of a cloned family member), adults' rights to procreative liberty, children's rights to privacy and equality, and commercial surrogacy. These are only a few of the areas of concern that can be related to human cloning. Some reports have also indicated that it is important to study the possible psychological and emotional state of individuals produced by cloning, the social aspects of their families, and the possible effects on society.

Emotional responses have dominated the debate on human cloning, and although emotions can sometimes be justified, many times they can be caused by prejudice.

In this [viewpoint], I argue that an individual created through the application of human cloning techniques, or other similar techniques, or any other type of genetic manipulation, will not show the donor's characteristics to the extent of compromising uniqueness. The creation of genetically identical individual/s will never lead to the replication of the donor's experiences. In addition, human experiences are not independent of space and time, and, since every human clone, or multiple clones, of an individual will be born in a unique context, cloned human beings' experiences will be unique in each case. Therefore, cloned individuals will be able to develop their own identities, their own personalities, and the uniqueness of any other human being. Furthermore, advances in biotechnology will offer human beings the possibility of enhancing their physical and cognitive abilities, as well as extending their life spans. These changes will not be able to take place without similar advances in the social sciences.

I also argue that a different approach to psychology is necessary to accompany the profound changes in society, and in the concept of human nature, that these biotechnological advances will bring. A new and different approach is imperative, in order to help human beings with new challenges and with the new mental processes they can be expected to face during a transition from a trans-human stage, which is already taking place on our planet, toward a future post-human stage that appears to be inevitable.

Criticism of Human Cloning

In regard to criticism of human cloning, [medical scholar Joshua] Lipschutz has suggested that the debate should not be labeled with a question about whether cloning is wrong, but rather with the question "When is cloning wrong?" Some of the objections to human cloning that have been presented are to the effect that it would have compromising effects on the welfare of the child. [Researchers J. Burley and J. Harris] describe the different forms of harm that, according to the critics of human cloning, a cloned child could suffer. The three types of harm they consider are:

1. Clones will be harmed by the prejudicial attitudes people may have towards them.
2. Clones will be harmed by the expectations and demands from parents or genotype donors.
3. Clones will be harmed by their own awareness of their origins.

In addition, Burley and Harris argue that the above objections to human cloning, based on child welfare, are misleading. They do not question the motivation of the objections, but consider that these formulations of the anti-cloning position do not provide a convincing argument. They do not deny that cloned individuals might indeed suffer some welfare deficits. However, they suggest, these deficits are not sufficient to warrant state interference with the choices of people who wish to clone their genes.

The debate should not be labeled with a question about whether cloning is wrong, but rather with the question "When is cloning wrong?"

From a standpoint very critical of human cloning, presented in testimony to the National Bioethics Advisory Commission on March 14, 1997, [physician] Leon R. Kass has questioned whether human procreation will remain human and whether children are going to be made rather than begotten. He suggests that "offensive," "grotesque," "revolting," "repugnant," and "repulsive" are the words most commonly heard in the street, and from intellectuals, believers, atheists, humanists, and scientists, regarding the prospect of human cloning.

Even though opposition to reproductive cloning is shared by many, the supporters of cloning have pointed out that the arguments presented by Kass are an emotional response to a new technology, and they do not provide a sufficient analysis of the risks, and the technology's benefits. In addition, according to [A.] Caplan, the arguments against cloning, endorsed by Leon Kass, Francis Fukuyama and others, are presented as if their authors hold the moral high ground in the public debate. Caplan suggests that these arguments are mostly based on pseudoscience, ideology, and plain fearmongering, which are then used to manipulate public opinion. . . .

Identity and Human Cloning

Among the critics of human cloning, [P.A.] Baird claims that human cloning presents a threat to our concepts of human identity and individuality. Baird argues that when a child of a particular genetic constitution is deliberately made, it is easier to consider the child as a product rather than a gift of providence. Kass also writes about some of the psychological consequences that a cloned human might experience in her/his life in society. He states that cloning will create serious issues of identity and individuality. According to Kass, a person who has been cloned may experience serious concerns about her or his identity, not only because of identical appearance to another human being, but because her identical twin might be her father or mother. In addition, Kass suggests that people in society will be prone to compare the performances of a cloned person with the performances of her alter ego.

However, according to Caplan, the arguments against cloning endorsed by Kass and other critics of human cloning are presented as if they possess the moral high ground in the public debate. Caplan argues that the arguments of Kass and others are, instead, mostly based on pseudoscience, ideology, and plain fearmongering, which are used to manipulate public opinion. [Researcher K.] Evers has also criticized the opponents of human cloning, and maintains that the concept of identity is ambiguous. Accordingly, the statement that cloning produces identical individuals is not meaningful, unless the concept is clarified.

Identity is defined as an organized conception of the self, in which the person can define his or her own values, goals, and beliefs. It is the immediate perception of one's selfsameness and continuity in time, with the simultaneous perception of the fact that others recognize one's sameness and continuity. Identity is also defined as a clearly expressed theory of oneself as someone who can act on the basis of reason, can explain her or his own behavior and own actions, and take responsibility for these actions. Identity is reached through a series of stages in life, and each of these is experienced differently by each individual during development and throughout the entire life span.

Identity is also the result of a continuous enriching process in which our entire personality acquires those individual characteristics that differentiate us from others.

The idea that creating another human being with exactly the same genotype would mean creating another human being with the same identity, and the same personality, is fundamentally wrong. At this point, the latter is impossible for us as human mortals. Furthermore, in the hypothetical case that scientists one day could create multiple human beings with exactly the same genotype, the creation of these genetically identical individuals would not lead to the production of individuals with the same identity and personality. The creation or production of human beings with the same personality, and without uniqueness, will not be possible, at least based on all the evidence from research on human beings with identical or nearly identical DNA. . . .

The effects of early experience on brain, body, mind, and behavior in newborns have been shown in different studies. Furthermore, empirical evidence confirms the role of experience in brain development of newborns. These studies demonstrate how experience induces changes in the developing brain shortly after birth, and how cognitive abilities differ in terms of neural plasticity [that is, the ability of the brain to change in response to experience] and the length of time during which experience can affect brain development.

Production of human beings with the same personality, and without uniqueness, will not be possible, at least based on all the evidence from research on human beings with identical or nearly identical DNA.

In terms of twin studies, no monozygotic [identical] twins are born at exactly the same time; and no clone of any person will come to life at the same time or occupy the same space as the person from whom he or she was cloned. Any difference in time and space could make an enormous difference with respect to the way any newborn, identical twins or eventually human clones, could be stimulated by the environment. As in the case of monozygotic twins, there will always be differences between human clones with respect to the time and space in which they will be born. These particular and small differences could lead to differences in novel experiences which will provide critical input into a nervous system, which in its turn would mean significant differences between these human clones in terms of how their brains will process new signals, and perceive subsequent novel stimuli. This will also lead to considerable differences in terms of self-concept, identity and personality development. . . .

Cloning Issues Should Be Treated as Reality

In 1997, Ian Wilmut and his associates at the Roslin Institute in Scotland announced the successful cloning of a sheep that they'd named "Dolly." The announcement created a debate regarding religious, legal, and ethical views on whether human cloning should be undertaken for the purposes of enhancing the quality of human life, and, if so, how it should be regulated.

There is awareness in the scientific community, including the medical community, that human cloning and the creation of clones are inevitable. There is also a belief that the medical community will one day have to address the care of and respect for people created by cloning techniques, and that the discussion of issues related to human cloning must begin now, before the first person born in this manner becomes fact.

Some scientists think that there should be more connection between the behavioral sciences and biology. Harvard University biologist Edward O. Wilson, for example, has long argued for a connection between biology and behavior. He states that psychologists can help bridge the natural and behavioral sciences and that psychology will play a critical role in unifying science during the twenty-first century. He also argues that the natural sciences, social sciences, and humanities are converging, and that their convergence will help solve many of the world's most afflictive problems. At the American Psychological Association's 2000 annual convention, Francis Collins, Human Genome Project director, suggested that psychologists would play an important role in genomics and genetics. He outlined the need for behavioral scientists to increase their involvement with, and to gain a greater mastery of, the field of genetics.

Human cloning and the creation of clones are inevitable.

The new advanced technologies, such as genetic engineering and human cloning, are bringing unprecedented challenges in terms of their behavioral, political, and ethical implications. These implications must be addressed on time, or society risks the consequences of an uncontrolled future. In other fields of learning, such as sociology, history, medicine, genetics, and philosophy, the issues concerning human cloning and its implications on human behavior have been a focus of study. Many scholars in these fields have pointed out the need for debate and discussed a variety of concerns relating to various aspects of human cloning that include psychological aspects and the perceptions and attitudes of the public.

New Ways of Thinking About Life

Research on human genetic engineering will facilitate human beings reaching another stage in history where all the expressions of science will be used to enhance our physical, social, emotional, and cognitive abilities. A civilization that uses genetic manipulation to enhance human beings' physical capabilities will make a transition to another stage in human evolution. This will be called a post-human stage, and is one in which psychology should play a very important role.

With all the changes that human cloning will precipitate, we may conclude that ideology and the convergence of natural sciences with the social sciences will play a fundamental role in the transition from a trans-human society, in which advances in physics, biotechnology and medicine will help the human race to overcome physical and social limitations that hinder humans in their search for harmony within the universe. Psychology should be a science that helps us to understand and incorporate any methods or technologies that help to enhance the physical and cognitive abilities of human beings. It is imperative for psychology to cooperate with other sciences for the incorporation of the responsible use of human cloning techniques, and the use of diverse biotechnological advances, genetic manipulation, and the development of therapies that have the potential to eliminate serious diseases that bring so much pain and suffering.

A civilization that uses genetic manipulation to enhance human beings' physical capabilities will make a transition to another stage in human evolution.

Advances in biotechnology will bring not only the possibility of using genetic manipulation for physical and mental augmentation. New techniques also have the potential to eliminate the need for organ transplants, and hence the corruption and crime involved in the illegal traffic of human organs. It may also alleviate the psychological suffering of childless couples, who are reluctant to initiate what is sometimes a long and emotionally conflictive adoption process. Advances in biotechnology, and more specifically in human cloning techniques, have countless applications from which humanity can obtain benefits. Contrary to what the critics of human cloning have stated, and paradoxically, the perfection of human cloning techniques could become a safe harbor for the preservation of the human species and the entire human genome. The perfection of human cloning techniques could provide the possibility to preserve and replicate the genetic code of a human being, as it is today, in the case that unwanted or unknown events could mutate, or threaten to mutate, a genomic region, or the entire human genome.

Obviously, for those who believe and trust that advances in science and biotechnology will bring only something positive to humanity, the hope is that human augmentation will help human beings to interact better with our environment and within this universe that we share with other living things. At that point, we will have reached a post-human stage. Human enhancement is a period of transition, a trans-human stage, in which humans will be able to enhance the capacity of their bodies, in order to cope better with the continuous demands of the environment, and which will bring human beings closer to becoming an integral part of the unity of this universe.

If we are to reach a post-human stage, all sciences—social sciences and natural sciences together—will have to work through a transitional period in which we recognize and accept that we have reached a point of no return in the course of human history on this planet. We have already started a transition, a trans-human stage, which we should consider a transition to a post-human stage, where humans will transcend their inherited body, with all its physical, social, emotional, and cognitive limitations, and convert it to an enhanced body, which will have more chance to deal with the continual pressures and demands of our rapidly developing human civilization.

Periodical and Internet Sources Bibliography

The following articles have been selected to supplement the diverse views presented in this chapter.

Antony Blackburn-Starza	"British Couple Successfully Screens Out Genetic Disorder Using NHS-Funded PGD," *BioNews*, June 9, 2008.
Satoshi Kanazawa	"Common Misconceptions About Science IV: Human Cloning," *Psychology Today*, March 15, 2009.
Brandon Keim	"Designer Babies: A Right to Choose?," *Wired*, March 9, 2009.
Jiro Nudeshima	"Human Cloning Legislation in Japan," *Eubios Journal of Asian and International Bioethics*, 2001.
Philippine Daily Inquirer	"Muslims Not Prepared to Declare Cloning 'Halal,'" June 26, 2008.
Danielle Simmons	"Genetic Inequality: Human Genetic Engineering," *Nature Education*, 2008.
Margaret Sleeboom-Faulkner	"Contested Embryonic Culture in Japan—Public Discussion, and Human Embryonic Stem Cell Research in an Aging Welfare Society," *Medical Anthropology*, vol. 29, no. 1, 2010.
Bob Sullivan	"Religions Reveal Little Consensus on Cloning," MSNBC, 2012. www.msnbc.msn.com.
Rebecca Tuhus-Dubrow	"Designer Babies and the Pro-Choice Movement," *Dissent*, Summer 2007.
Hilary White	"Overwhelming Support in Ireland for Law Protecting Human Embryos," LifeSiteNews, June 10, 2010. www.lifesitenews.com.

For Further Discussion

Chapter 1

1. Henry Miller refers to anti–genetic modification regulation as "discriminatory regulation." What might be the purpose of linking the anti-GM movement to discrimination? What is the rhetorical effect when Gathuru Mburu says that Kenyans need a food policy that "liberates rather than enslaves" them?

2. In the viewpoint by Lan Lan, Monsanto says that its crops are drought resistant. In the viewpoint by Pete Riley and his colleagues, the authors claim that Monsanto's crops are not especially drought resistant. Who makes the better case in your view? Explain your reasoning.

Chapter 2

1. Based on the viewpoint in this chapter, is the Consumers Association of Penang justified in believing that genetically engineered mosquitoes might have devastating unintended consequences? Back up your opinion by discussing the viewpoints by Gunther Latsch, Jian J. Duan and colleagues, and Sarah Cumberland.

2. Based on the viewpoint by Jerry Warner and his colleagues, what should the United States do to reduce the threat of biowarfare? Explain your reasoning.

Chapter 3

1. If cloning is cruel to animals, should it be used to preserve endangered species? Explain your reasoning based on the viewpoints by the International Coalition for Animal Welfare and Raul E. Piña-Aguilar and his colleagues.

Chapter 4

1. Should human embryos be treated differently in different cultures? Is a particular public's view of these issues significant, or do the same moral laws govern these issues no matter what the culture? Use the viewpoints by Kevin Doran, Satoshi Kodama and Akira Akabayashi, and Abdulaziz Sachedina to support your argument.

2. Does the viewpoint by Nestor Micheli Morales convince you that human cloning should be allowed if the technology becomes available? Based on Morales's arguments and the rest of the viewpoints in this chapter, do traditional moral frameworks become obsolete with the introduction of new technology? Explain your reasoning.

Organizations to Contact

The editors have compiled the following list of organizations concerned with the issues debated in this book. The descriptions are derived from materials provided by the organizations. All have publications or information available for interested readers. The list was compiled on the date of publication of the present volume; the information provided here may change. Be aware that many organizations take several weeks or longer to respond to inquiries, so allow as much time as possible.

Council for Responsible Genetics (CRG)
5 Upland Road, Suite 3, Cambridge, MA   02140
(617) 868-0870 • fax: (617) 491-5344
e-mail: crg@gene-watch.org
website: www.gene-watch.org

Council for Responsible Genetics (CRG) works to provide accurate and current information about emerging biotechnologies so that citizens can play a more active role in shaping policies regarding these advances. Specific topics addressed by the organization include genetic determinism, cloning and human genetic manipulation, and constructing and promoting a "Genetic Bill of Rights." *GeneWatch* is the bimonthly publication of CRG. Articles from this magazine as well as other institute reports are accessible on the CRG website.

Friends of the Earth International (FOEI)
PO Box 19199, Amsterdam   1000 GD
    The Netherlands
31 20 622 1369 • fax: 31 20 639 2181
website: www.foei.org

Friends of the Earth International (FOEI) is an international grassroots environmental network. Its member organizations campaign worldwide for food sovereignty, economic justice, and biodiversity, among other environmental and social justice issues. The organization opposes the use of genetically modified (GM) crops as environmentally and economically dangerous. Its website includes news releases, reports, and numerous other publications and resources.

Greenpeace

702 H Street NW, Suite 300, Washington, DC 20001
(202) 462-1177 • fax: (202) 462-4507
e-mail: info@wdc.greenpeace.org
website: www.greenpeace.org

Greenpeace is an activist group seeking to protect the environment worldwide. Current focuses of the organization include combating global warming, deforestation, and ocean pollution. Additionally, Greenpeace opposes the genetic engineering (GE) of food and food sources, and contends that any GE food on the market should be labeled. Reports on the threat of genetic engineering to the environment, as well as articles on other topics, can be downloaded from the Greenpeace website.

Institute of Science in Society (ISIS)

29 Tytherton Road, London N19 4PZ
England
+44 (0) 1908 696101
e-mail: jules@i-sis.org.uk
website: www.i-sis.org.uk

The Institute of Science in Society (ISIS) is a not-for-profit organization dedicated to providing critical and accessible scientific information to the public and to promoting social accountability and ecological sustainability in science. ISIS provides scientific advice to the Third World Network, a nongovernmental organization based in Penang, Malaysia. It also runs training programs about genetic engineering in developing countries and elsewhere, and produces scientific papers on topics such as genetic engineering. ISIS argues for greater public input and more caution in the use of genetic engineering with crops. ISIS publishes the quarterly magazine *Science in Society*, as well as other publications and reports, all of which are available through its website.

Monsanto

800 N. Lindbergh Boulevard, St. Louis, MO   63167
(314) 694-1000
website: www.monsanto.com

Monsanto is a multinational agribusiness biotechnology corporation. It is the world's leading producer of genetically engineered seed and a major producer of herbicides. Its website includes information about its products, news releases, and discussions of issues relating to agribusiness such as genetically modified crops.

National Human Genome Research Institute (NHGRI)

Communications and Public Liaison Branch
National Human Genome Research Institute
National Institutes of Health, Building 31, Room 4B09
Bethesda, MD   20892-2152
(301) 402-0911 • fax: (301) 402-2218
website: www.genome.gov

The National Human Genome Research Institute (NHGRI) is a branch of the National Institutes of Health in the United States that was established in 1989 to participate in the International Human Genome Project. Since the completion of the sequencing of the human genome, NHGRI has embarked on the mission of further researching the genome to better understand how it functions in human health and disease. Additionally, NHGRI provides information about policy and ethics issues as well as educational material about human genetics. Detailed information about these and other topics can be searched and viewed on the NHGRI website.

Nuffield Council on Bioethics

28 Bedford Square, London   WC1B 3JS
    England

(020) 7681 9619 • fax: (020) 7637 1712
e-mail: bioethics@nuffieldbioethics.org
website: www.nuffieldbioethics.org

Established in 1991, the Nuffield Council on Bioethics works to identify and address ethical issues connected with current and emerging biotechnologies. The council also provides educational information to the public to stimulate discussion and debate about these technologies. The Nuffield Council's website offers papers the council has published, including "The Ethics of Patenting DNA, Genetically Modified Crops: Ethical and Social Issues" and "Stem Cell Therapy: Ethical Issues."

US Department of Homeland Security (DHS)
Washington, DC   20528
(202) 282-8000
website: www.dhs.gov/index.shtm

Created just after the September 11, 2001, terrorist attacks on the United States, the US Department of Homeland Security (DHS) was envisioned as a central agency that could coordinate federal, state, and local resources to prevent or respond to threats to the American homeland. The DHS website contains speeches and congressional testimony by DHS representatives, in addition to mission statements and department performance records. Many of these documents relate to the dangers of bioterrorism and the development of biological weapons.

US Food and Drug Administration (FDA)
10903 New Hampshire Avenue, Silver Spring, MD   20993
888-463-6332
website: www.fda.gov

The Food and Drug Administration (FDA) is the US government agency responsible for ensuring the quality and safety of all food and drug products sold in the United States. As such, the FDA has conducted extensive tests to evaluate the safety of genetically engineered (GE) foods and has issued guidelines and regulatory measures to control what types of GE products make it to market. The Center for Veterinary Medicine (CVM), an office within the FDA, specifically examines the impact of GE products on animals and has also researched and reported on the cloned animals that will be used in the food industry. Reports by both the FDA and CVM can be retrieved from the FDA website.

World Health Organization (WHO)

Avenue Appia 20, Geneva 27   1211
   England
+41 22 791 21 11 • fax: +41 22 791 31 11
e-mail: postmaster@paho.org
website: www.who.int

The World Health Organization (WHO) is an agency of the United Nations formed in 1948 with the goal of creating and ensuring a world where all people can live with high levels of both mental and physical health. The organization researches and endorses different methods of combating the spread of diseases such as malaria, SARS, and deadly strains of influenza. WHO publishes the *Bulletin of the World Health Organization*, which is available online, as well as the *Pan American Journal of Public Health*. Its website includes numerous reports and discussions of genetically modified foods and other genetic engineering and biotechnology issues.

Bibliography of Books

John C. Avise | *The Hope, Hype, and Reality of Genetic Engineering: Remarkable Stories from Agriculture, Industry, Medicine, and the Environement.* New York: Oxford University Press, 2004.

T.A. Brown | *Gene Cloning and DNA Analysis: An Introduction.* 6th ed. Hoboken, NJ: Wiley-Blackwell, 2010.

Claire Hope Cummings | *Uncertain Peril: Genetic Engineering and the Future of Seeds.* Boston, MA: Beacon Press, 2008.

F. William Engdahl | *Seeds of Destruction: The Hidden Agenda of Genetic Manipulation.* Montreal, Quebec: Global Research, 2007.

Nina V. Fedoroff and Nancy Marie Brown | *Mendel in the Kitchen: A Scientist's View of Genetically Modified Foods.* Washington, DC: Joseph Henry Press, 2004.

Sakiko Fukuda-Parr, ed. | *The Gene Revolution: GM Crops and Unequal Development.* Sterling, VA: Earthscan, 2007.

Jeanne Guillemin | *American Anthrax: Fear, Crime, and the Investigation of the Nation's Deadliest Bioterror Attack.* New York: Times Books, 2011.

Jeanne Guillemin — *Biological Weapons: From the Invention of State-Sponsored Programs to Contemporary Bioterrorism.* New York: Columbia University Press, 2005.

Christine Mummery, Ian Wilmut, Anja Van De Stolpe, and Bernard Roelen — *Stem Cells: Scientific Facts and Fiction.* Burlington, MA: Academic Press, 2011.

Desmond S.T. Nicholl — *An Introduction to Genetic Engineering.* New York: Cambridge University Press, 2008.

Alice Park — *The Stem Cell Hope: How Stem Cell Medicine Can Change Our Lives.* New York: Hudson Street Press, 2011.

G. Pfleiderer, G. Brahier, and K. Lindpaintner, eds. — *GenEthics and Religion.* Basel, Switzerland: Karger, 2010.

Jeffrey R. Ryan and Jan F. Glarum — *Biosecurity and Bioterrorism: Containing and Preventing Biological Threats.* Boston, MA: Butterworth-Heinemann, 2008.

Michael J. Sandel — *The Case Against Perfection: Ethics in the Age of Genetic Engineering.* Cambridge, MA: Belknap Press, 2007.

Michael Schacker — *A Spring Without Bees: How Colony Collapse Disorder Has Endangered Our Food Supply.* Guilford, CT: Lyons Press, 2008.

Richard Sherlock   *Nature's End: The Theological Meaning of the New Genetics.* Wilmington, DE: ISI Books, 2010.

Lee M. Silver   *Remaking Eden: How Genetic Engineering and Cloning Will Transform the American Family.* New York: Avon Books, 1997.

Amy E. Smithson   *Germ Gambits: The Bioweapons Dilemma, Iraq and Beyond.* Stanford, CA: Stanford University Press, 2011.

Reece Walters   *Eco Crime and Genetically Modified Food.* New York: Routledge, 2011.

John Woestendiek   *Dog, Inc.: The Uncanny Inside Story of Cloning Man's Best Friend.* New York: Avery, 2010.

Index

Geographic headings and page numbers in **boldface** refer to viewpoints about that country or region.

.